How to
Write
Science
Fiction

JAN

How to Write Science Fiction

Matthew J. Costello

MARLOWE & COMPANY
New York

Second edition, 1995

Published in the United States by

Marlowe & Company
632 Broadway, Seventh Floor
New York, N.Y. 10012

Library of Congress Cataloging-in-Publication Data

Costello, Matthew J.
    How to write science fiction / Matthew J. Costello.— 2nd ed.
        p.   cm.
    Includes bibliographical refences.
    ISBN 1-56924-844-3
    1. Science fiction—Authorship.   I. Title.
PN3377.5.S3C65   1995
808.3'8762—dc20   91-43471
                                                              CIP

Manufactured in the United States of America

To my brother Michael—who also has been known to give some good advice.

Contents

CONTENTS

Part 3: Storytelling and SF

Part 4: The Business of Writing

Introduction

MAKE no mistake about it. There are two very different kinds of readers of science fiction.

One person picks up a novel by Isaac Asimov, or Arthur C. Clarke, or Robert Heinlein, and gets lost in a wondrous vision of a future.

And, after finishing the book, that reader puts it down, excited and eager to start a new book, to read George Alec Effinger, perhaps, or Orson Scott Card . . . to continue their fascination with speculative fiction.

Then there is a completely different type of reader, someone who picks up a book like this, someone, perhaps, like you. . . .

Maybe you have felt differently about reading science fiction for a *long* time. With each book completed, each short story devoured, a powerful desire grew inside you to *join* the creators, to become a writer.

Sometimes this determination can spring from simple admiration. In other cases, after a disappointing book, you might have the nagging feeling that you could do better.

Whatever it is, the idea grows . . .

I want to write science fiction. I have stories to tell. *I want to do this too.*

If you're lucky, that feeling passes.

Because—and consider this fair warning—it's not easy to join the ranks of published authors. And once there, the new writer soon discovers that a world of struggle and yearning opens up before them.

But you've bought this book—and you've read this far. You won't be deterred that easily . . .

What are the prerequisites for proceeding? You want to write science fiction. You've read widely in the field, and you know what kind of stories you enjoy. You have favorite authors.

And possibly you've done some writing. You've written some short stories, maybe even started a novel. Perhaps you've even sent a story out to a magazine or two, and have already tasted rejection.

It's a dish all professional authors get to know well.

And there's this—you have an irresistible urge to tell stories. That urge, the desire to tell tales, will be hard to manufacture if it's not inside you already.

With this foundation—unafraid of rejection, and blessed, or cursed, with an urge to tell tales—you've picked up this book . . .

Now, before we begin, you deserve to hear of your instructor's background, and where exactly I plan on taking you.

I've published over a dozen books, more than half of

which have been science fiction. I've written books set in the fantastic worlds created by Robert Silverberg and Robert Heinlein. My novel *The Wizard of Tizare*—set on a world of intelligent cat-like creatures, the Mrem—was a Waldenbooks bestseller, and the first two volumes of my *Time Warrior* trilogy have recently been published by NAL/ROC. My recent novels *Midsummer* and *Wurm* (Berkley/Diamond) are both thrillers with strong science fiction elements.

And though I'm not a terribly active short story writer—I just don't have the time to steal from my books—I've had stories in anthologies dealing with time travel (*Time Gate II,* edited by Robert Silverberg), a futuristic Robin Hood (*Fantastic Robin Hood,* edited by Martin Greenberg) and unsolved mysteries (*Solved!,* edited by Martin Greenberg and Ed Gorman).

I'm an Editorial Associate for the Writer's Digest School, where I've worked with hopeful writers in the science fiction and horror fields. Some of the advice you'll read here first appeared, in a different form, in the pages of *Writer's Digest*.

Be warned: I will unabashedly refer to my own work to detail the processes that I went through in creating my worlds and characters. I'll explain the type of research I did to get the science right for my fiction, and the way I put together plot and characters to create an intelligible story.

But more importantly, I'll show you, step by step, how to create a believable science fiction world and characters for your story and novel. We'll look at the different types of science fiction, and the style and approach each demands.

There are sections on how to construct a world, getting your science right, and how to avoid the hoary clichés of SF that have had their day.

Award-winning writers in the field, such as Orson Scott Card and Jane Yolen, will describe how they work and what the future might hold for writers of science fiction.

How To Write Science Fiction also includes a guide to selling science fiction. There are lists of important conventions to attend, the major publishing houses that have regular science fiction lines, and the magazines you simply must read to stay current in the field.

I'll help you craft a professional-looking proposal, with a look at the submission guidelines used for one publisher's science fiction series. Making your manuscript or proposal as professional as possible is the way to get past the first editorial hurdle.

And then—should you make a sale—I'll give you some advice on how to be your own agent (and why you most certainly don't need—or want—one now).

We'll look at other markets for science fiction writing, such as film, television, comic book and role-playing games, and the future of science fiction. The future of science fiction may lie in unlikely markets such as computer games and CD-ROM, where interactive movies written by science fiction authors will become a reality.

But first—before we go any further—let's make sure that we all we agree on what exactly is *science fiction* . . .

CHAPTER
1

What Is (and Isn't) Science Fiction?

In 1991, the members of the Science Fiction Writers Association (SFWA) became embroiled in a controversy that threatened to split the organization of professional writers completely apart.

Various writers in the organization wished to change the bylaws and establish *eight* different categories of membership, depending on just how active a writer was . . . and what exactly they had published. Some argued that only works of *real* science fiction should qualify an author for membership.

The controversy provoked a tidal wave of letters from long-standing members protesting not only the bureaucracy that managing such a system would entail—deciding what's an eligible book or not—but also the inequity of penalizing writers who, for one reason or another, hadn't made a sale in a while.

Some members threatened to quit the organization, while others defended the eight-tiered system. The battle, still raging, continues to be fought in the SFWA members-only publication, *The Forum*.

It raised, once again, a question that has plagued sience fiction from the days of Jules Verne and H.G. Wells.

What exactly is science fiction?

To the general reader, science fiction is something futuristic, often with scientific or pseudo-scientific devices that don't yet exist and, in all likelihood, never will. Sometimes there are aliens and strange worlds, or star ships and time machines.

Weird, wacky stuff . . . as Johnny Carson might observe.

But that simple description belies the host of subcategories in the field today.

There is *hard* science fiction, stories and novels that deal with real technology projected to its logical conclusions. Hard science fiction writers do a lot of research to get that science right. There's no kidding around here, and sometimes the human story can take a back seat to the technological possibilities being considered.

John W. Campbell, Jr., famed editor of the science fiction magazine *Astounding/Analog* from the late thirties to 1971, and author of the chilling story "Who Goes There?," was a important editor, writer and advocate of hard SF.

And then, at the other extreme, there is Space Opera. Robert Heinlein's book *Have Space Suit—Will Travel* and George Lucas' Flash Gordon-inspired film, *Star Wars*, with its empire, rebels, togas, and noisy space ships, is a good example of this type of flamboyant science fiction.

In space opera the human story is important, though the characters may be drawn in broad strokes of good and evil. The feats of interstellar derring-do may be more appropriate on a pirate ship than a star cruiser.

Cyberpunk is a recent division in the field, fueled by the rapidly changing micro-technology of computers and communications. William Gibson's *Neuromancer*, about a data thief who can link his mind with a world-spanning computer, is a key cyberpunk work. George Alec Effinger's *When Gravity Fails*, another seminal cyberpunk novel, takes place in a marvelously seedy Arab underworld where people "chip" into their brain mood-altering computer "middies." In cyberpunk, the human and the computer are on intimate terms, with chips attached to the cerebral cortex.

At the same time, the cyberpunk world can be impersonal, dangerous, and unmanageable—not much different from everyday life in cities today. Cyberpunk often has a grim outlook on the future, set to a pounding rock soundtrack.

Many science fiction novels, and writers, can be defined by their themes, by what they choose to write about. Some science fiction writers deal with alien worlds, removed from earthly concerns. Others deal very much with Earth, facing problems such as overpopulation, environmental disasters, and the assorted holes in the ozone layer.

Time travel, my favorite theme, is virtually a subgenre in itself, with modern classics like David Gerrold's *The Boy Who Folded Himself*. Military science fiction is popular, especially the novels of David Drake (*Hammer's Slammers*) and Joe Haldeman (*The Forever War*).

Alternate histories—the South won the Civil War . . . and Hitler survived the bunker to open a theme park in Argentina . . . and JFK was with Marilyn the morning Lee Oswald got fed up with his life—are great fun and a rich vein for science fiction writers. Even mainstream authors have trouble resisting the lure of alternate histories, as witness Len Deighton's *SS-GB*, his novel of the Nazi occupation of Great Britain.

Other key science fiction themes include post-apocalyptic tales, books like Stephen King's *The Stand* or Harlan Ellison's *A Boy and His Dog*. Fable and satire, such as Douglas Adams' *A Hitchiker's Guide to the Galaxy* and Terry Pratchett's *Discworld*, also attract a loyal core of readers.

There are also endless robot stories, utopia tales, idea stories that deal with one striking concept, and a host of what-if stories.

Then there is fantasy . . . with its dragons and wizards, fantastic planets, and interstellar weirdness that defies *all* concepts of science.

And here battle lines can be drawn.

What is science fiction, and what is fantasy? Where, for example, does *Lord Valentine's Castle*, and Majipoor, Robert Silverberg's planet of sea monsters and shape-changing aliens, fit?

One argument is that real science fiction has to deal with the recognizable universe, obeying the laws of that universe, projecting history and scientific development in a realistic way.

But that's easier said than done. Who's to know what holds true in other solar systems, in other parts of the universe? Fantasy, on the other hand, doesn't concern itself with explanations for wondrous things. Much of what is labeled "fantasy" eschews the sometimes lengthy technical background favored by the hard science fiction writer.

And many great science fiction writers, such as Harlan Ellison and Ray Bradbury, often write fantastic stories with nary a concern for the rules of *science* fiction.

Science fiction has grown from the days of Jules Verne's Nautilus in *Twenty Thousand Leagues Under the Sea* and H.G. Wells' grim future in *The Time Machine*. Many writers have accepted labeling the field SF, to stand for "speculative fiction." SF embraces the entire field, from the most imaginative and fantastic world creations—the weirdest alien adventure—to those that are heavily researched and realistic—the heavily scientific techno-adventures.

If we need a label, SF will do as well as any.

What's important is for you, the writer, to decide what *you* want to write about. To do that, you'll need a story, of course, and characters. But before that, there must come a world.

You must create your world, with your vision and your coherent rules.

And here's where we get to work . . .

Part 1:

BUILDING
YOUR
WORLD

CHAPTER
2

World-Building by the Masters

Before you create your story, before you even *try* to breathe life into a cast of characters, you must create a world. Without a believable and compelling world—a special organization of natural and created things—your story and characters can never be convincing to the reader.

In SF, the medium is often the message. Make the world a place of depth, of history, and then whatever amazing things take place there will have the possibility of being believed.

Your "world" doesn't have to be some distant star-system, with planets with bizarre ecosystems. It could very well be here and now. Whether it's the block you live on or a complex civilization light years away, your created world is the grounding, the underpinning to your work—especially if you'll be writing SF.

And there's no better way to learn world-building than to look at three worlds created by three masters.

Silverberg's Majipoor

Robert Silverberg's *Lord Valentine's Castle* (1980) marked his dramatic return to science fiction after a long hiatus when—as he described it in his introduction to my book, *Revolt on Majipoor* (1987)—"I was busy traveling, and reading, and constructing an elaborate exotic garden at my northern California home."

But then he was struck with an idea, an image of a *place*. He wrote the idea on the back of an envelope . . .

"The scene is a giant planet-sized city—an urban Big Planet, population of billions . . . the city is divided into vast sub-cities, each with its own characteristic tone."

Silverberg went on to sketch out the romantic story of the book, about Lord Valentine, who has had his identity stolen and is imprisoned in another body. But the key thing to note here is that this world appeared first.

What about plot and character?

In upcoming chapters we'll discuss plot, but, trust me, the stories and the themes of the tales you want to tell will not vary much from genre to genre. You may feature robots, artificial intelligence, and time travel but your stories will still be about love and hate, loss and revenge.

It's your world creation that will lay the special groundwork for your themes and subtext.

After this initial inspiration, Silverberg soon amended his concept of his planet. He realized it couldn't just be one enormous city, so it became a *planet* of enormous cities, with forests, valleys, mountains, deserts, and giant seas.

But if a planet was so large, then its gravitational pull would be crushing. Silverberg solved this by making the planet, Majipoor, have a very light core, with little in the way of metals.

From the size of the planet, Silverberg had determined that it was metal-poor—and therefore could not have a traditional high technology. It could still have advanced communications and its own unique form of transportation.

With a rough idea of the planet, Silverberg created the history. Majipoor, he decided, was created by colonists from Earth some fourteen thousand years before the events documented in his novel. But the earthlings arrived on a planet occupied by six strange, intelligent races.

There were Skandars, who resemble six-limbed bears . . . and Ghayrogs, reptile-like creatures with Medusa-like hair. Vroons were much like land-going octopuses gifted with telepathic powers; Liimen, like three-eyed humanoids. The Hjorts were chubby gray creatures with bulbous frog eyes.

The strangest group of all, the Piurivars—also known as the Metamorphs—are the mysterious native race of Majipoor. They are shape-shifters, and they are feared by all the other races.

For each group, Silverberg created a biological and social structure. For example, the Hjorts are often in positions of minor authority, while the Ghayrogs show emotion through odor.

Silverberg's background for his world also included the

flora and fauna, including the vicious mouth plants, fire-shower trees, singing ferns, cow-like blaves, spinner birds, and a host of other animals and plants.

Majipoor is made up of four continents, and Silverberg provides a rich background for each. We learn that Alhanroel has the important governmental center at Castle Mount, while Zimroel holds the Metamorph reservation.

The governmental system is also detailed. The Pontifex is the mysterious imperial ruler of the planet—and no one speaks directly to him. The Coronal is the chief administrator of the planet, and heir to the Pontifex.

Religion is important on the planet, with The Lady of the Isle of Sleep presiding over the spiritual life of Majipoor.

There are assorted aspects of this great and wonderful world we learn about, such as the weapons (energy throwers and vibrating swords), the recreation (entertainment cubes), and travel (floaters). And this only scratches the surface—excuse the pun—of Majipoor.

Simply learning of all these things piques our interest. The place, the grand world of Majipoor, is exciting and compelling. Before we know any characters or any plot, we are involved in the story because of the wonders of Silverberg's world.

Heinlein's Glory Road

Robert A. Heinlein's *Glory Road* (1963) is really a sword-and-sorcery tale with science fiction underpinnings. The novel starts in the Riviera, with a bored ex-soldier, Easy Gordon, who gets called on to perform tremendous acts of heroism in the twenty alternate universes reached by means of the Glory Road.

Heinlein's conceit in the book is that there are Twenty Universes, alternate views of reality. And he fills those universes with dragons, lightning creatures, antigravity zones, and monster "Constructs."

Where Silverberg is tremendously detailed about his giant planet, Majipoor, Heinlein is sketchy about the worlds and about the pathway, the Glory Road, used to reach them. But as with so many created universes, we accept the fact that we can only glimpse bits and pieces of each, and so we accept Heinlein's creation, embrace it, and hang on for the ride.

The key here lies in the initial set-up of the book, the first "alternate universe" that we see. Easy Gordon's world is *our* world—a familiar one, if you've ever been to Europe or the Riviera. Heinlein brings it vibrantly to life, with the beach, the sun, the smell of the restaurants, the hotels, and the streets. This realm is the location where Easy Gordon is lured, by an attractive woman, to leave Earth to save the Twenty Universes.

Heinlein starts the novel in our recognizable world, with a sympathetic character, so that we willingly accept the multiple universes he lays before us.

And though none of these alternate worlds is tremendously detailed, each is rich with exotic creatures and physical rules, and each has its own quirky nature—from universes where gravity has tenuous hold, to places where magic has replaced technology.

John W. Campbell's *Who Goes There?*

You won't find John Campbell's novella *Who Goes There?* listed under his own name. For this, his most famous story, Campbell, an editor who influenced an entire generation of science fiction writers, used the pseudonym "Don A. Stuart."

The story is the basis for two film versions titled *The Thing* (1951 and 1982). Most people assume that the second, more graphic version, directed by John Carpenter—with masterful special effects by Rob Bottin—was not a faithful adaptation. It differed in such a shocking way from the classic black-and-white film of the fifties.

But a reading of Campbell's tense novella shows that the second filmed version is true to his grisly story of an ambitious alien that can mimic any form of life. Here, Campbell used a method similar to Heinlein's in bringing us to accept the fantastic events that are to occur.

The action is set in a Research Station in Antarctica. Campbell never went to Antarctica. But by the way we can feel the icy wind and feel the isolation—you can be sure that Campbell, a trained engineer, researched the climate and environment of the frozen desert that is Antarctica.

Campbell's research station rings true, from its construction and layout to the concern for heating and food supply. The interaction of the station's military and scientific crew is easy and naturalistic, even as a dark tension overtakes the base in the presence of the intruding alien.

To a large extent, Campbell turned this location on earth into another world. He needed the isolation to make this battle against a powerful and opportunistic alien a vital stand for mankind. The story benefits immensely from the severity of the climate, and the very alien nature of so much cold and ice.

It seems, here, that the creature, the "thing," is more at home in the frozen climate than the warm-blooded humans.

One scene, in particular, deserves mention. It appears both in the novella and Carpenter's film. After the alien has penetrated the station, a test is devised, a blood test—a scene which sends long, ominous shadows onto these years of AIDS and paranoia.

The station crew gives small samples of their blood which will be subjected to an electric shock. The idea is that the alien's blood will recoil—since every part of it can act independently.

The scene is terrifying and grotesque, a shocking scene almost more appropriate to a horror novel. But the *reality* of the station, the crew's quarters, the labs, the mess hall, has been carefully established. So—when the test comes—we sense the three-dimensional reality of the setting, the petri dishes, the blood, and then—the payoff—the shocking response of the blood samples.

The same scene set on an alien world or a spaceship could not have been nearly as successful.

Studying Author's Worlds

I picked these three worlds not because they're the greatest worlds in science fiction—though they are marvelous creations. You'd certainly have to count, among the greatest worlds, Frank Herbert's giant desert, *Dune*, and the far-flung empire of Isaac Asimov's *Foundation* trilogy.

But the three worlds I've discussed are all worlds that I have worked with. And it was this work which helped me when it came time to create my own worlds.

My book, *Revolt on Majipoor* (1988), set in Silverberg's Majipoor, is an interactive novel, for Tor Books. In order to work in Silverberg's universe, I read his books *Lord Valentine's Castle* and *The Majipoor Chronicles*, pen in hand, taking notes on each aspect of the world.

I then covered file folders with a grid of 32 boxes, with columns for the plant life, the animals, the weapons and assorted objects to be found on the planet.

In each box, I drew a picture of the item, as I imagined it. (And make no mistake about it—I'm no artist, but my quick, rough sketch helped burn into my mind exactly what the object was like.)

Large features, such as the massive towers of the city of Dulorn and the Wooden Shacks in Narabal, were sketched on separate sheets.

For each race found on Majipoor, I drew a large color sketch, with words beneath it describing any physical or personality features not readily visible in my rough drawing.

I drew maps of the planet's four continents, marking all the major physical features, the rivers, the woods, and the mountain ranges, as well as the large cities and ports. A large map showed the relationship of the four continents to each other.

And when I knew where I wanted to set the action of my book, I prepared a detailed, bird's-eye map showing close-ups of physical features, such as lakes and trails, as well as important buildings.

By the time I began thinking about my plot and characters, I could look around my office and see pictures of Silverberg's bladder trees and the mouth plants. I could follow my hero's journey on the six maps. The gloomy, amateurishly drawn faces of the Metamorphs looked down on me when I considered what their special role was to be in the coming revolt on the giant planet.

Fate's Trick (1989) is an interactive novel set in Heinlein's twenty universes of *Glory Road*. And while I had a freer hand here, with so many alternate realities, I still prepared grids detailing the wonders of the various universes, as well as the short descriptions of the specific worlds Easy Gordon reaches.

Mapping here was less important—with twenty universes to deal with, a real map would be completely impossible. Still, I did draw maps of key locations and created new locations to fit the needs of my plot.

But like Heinlein's, my book starts in a very earthly location. Alex Tannen, an army buddy of Easy Gordon, is a stage magician performing in Sarasota, Florida, and, at the book's opening, he's not doing too well. Tannen gets summoned by the beautiful Palina and her little brother Tam, to help Easy "save the whole ball of wax—all twenty universes."

Alex has to make his jump to the Glory Road in the Everglades. In this case, I had actually been to the Everglades. I had walked its trails and studied the animals; I had maps of the National Park and books on its natural history. But I could also write about the swamp, and the alligators and cormorants, with the air and senses of someone who's been there.

When Alex is attacked in the swamp and falls off the wooden walkway, the reader believes in the location. This translates into a belief in the universes Alex must visit.

Like Campbell's *Who Goes There?*, my novel *Midsummer* (1990) is set in Antarctica. And no, I haven't been *there*. But Antarctica has long been an intense interest of mine. I have a shelf of books on the exploration of the frozen continent, from big coffee-table tomes and histories of the continent's explorers to the diaries of Scott's desperate attempt to be the first to the South Pole and the multinational Trans-Antarctic expedition of 1990.

I corresponded with the National Science Foundation about its base in McMurdo. I filled one wall with a giant map of Antarctica, marking the exact location of *my* research station, and where a certain strange discovery would be made. I researched the temperature range and windspeed, and its effect on everything from snowmobiles to helicopters.

I drew pictures of the types of snowmobiles used, from

the big tractors to the smaller one-man Cats. I obtained photos of Antarctic clothing, and learned about the problems connected with perspiration and weather vapor in a place where moisture freezes instantaneously.

I charted the dizzying variety of snow and ice, describing the "sastrugi"—frozen waves of ice—and crevasses. I read about glaciers and the Antarctic mountain ranges. I studied human psychology under the extreme conditions and isolation of Antarctic base.

Before I wrote one word of the prologue to *Midsummer*—set in the middle of the dark Antarctic winter—I absorbed as much information about the continent as I could, from the life cycle of the continent's wingless flies (the only indigenous land animals) to the feeding habits of the killer whales that hunt the ice floes for careless penguins.

And only then I was ready to write about one scientist—and what he finds way below the ice . . .

Exercise 1

In the next chapter, you'll design a world from the bottom up. But a good way to prepare to do that is to see how a professional author has done the same thing.

Pick a story or a novel by a SF author you admire. Read it, pen in hand, jotting down all the inventions of plants, animals, social customs, physical features, transportation and communications—everything that is unique to the author's world.

Then make a grid, and place the different things from the world onto it, in appropriate groups. Sketch any novel creatures or races, using the author's description to guide you. Map out key locations in the world, or special buildings or places where pivotal action takes place.

When you're done, look over the list to see if there seem to be key things left out. Has the food supply been neglected, or communication systems? How about religious beliefs, or mythology? Is there a history to the world, and does it explains the current societal set-up?

Seeing the components of an author's world in front of you will help you create your own. You should feel, after this exercise, that you could, in fact, write a story set in the author's world.

Creating a world can seem like a daunting process. In the next chapter, we'll approach it step by step, piecing together the components that will make your story and characters come to life.

CHAPTER
3

A Step-by-Step Guide To
Making Your World

George Alec Effinger's Budayeen would be an amazing place to visit. Featured in Effinger's *When Gravity Fails* and *A Fire in the Sun*, the Budayeen is an Arabian ghetto set on a future earth where you can chip in a "middie" to change your personality or a "daddie" to simply alter your mood.

Effinger's character, Marid Audran, is a street hustler turned unlikely policeman. It's through his eyes that we see the clubs, the streets and the back alleys of this intriguing world.

Of course, George Alec Effinger is a master storyteller. But his story wouldn't be nearly as absorbing and powerful if his world didn't ring absolutely true. George eventually went on to write a state-of-the-art computer game (for Infocom/Activision) set in his world. Called Circuit's Edge, it's "a gritty, fairly authentic visit to the world I created," he told me.

But before the world of the Budayeen was created in his novels and the graphic intrigue of a computer game, the

Budayeen existed in the author's mind. And that is the first step in crafting compelling SF.

In *The Wizard of Tizare* (1990), my novel about the cat-like Mrem, a whole world needed to be brought to life. The rough sketches needed to be filled out in detail. For example, here's a scene from the novel:

> Falon pulled his lined cape closer, pulling it tight against the thin fur at his throat. The herdbeasts, just below him, milling about in a flat, open piece of ground, didn't seem any happier. The lead buck shifted back and forth, as though to stir too much would only make it colder.
>
> Falon knew the feeling. If he moved, his cape let in tiny pockets of air. To stay still was to feel as frozen as one of the greyish-green clumps of rock that dotted the mountainside.

At first glance, it might seem that there are only two SF elements in the paragraph . . . the fact that Falon has fur, and the grazing herdbeasts. But the two paragraphs present a consistent world. Anyone who has ever thrown a cat out into the cold night knows how sleekly discomfited they can look. The cat walks away gingerly, as if afraid of the icy air.

Then there are the other details. We're reading about a mountain, an icy wind, an uncomfortable herd, weathered rocks. These have to come to life for the reader.

And—here's the secret—if they do, so will the rest of the world, like the animal called a Rar . . . a lumbering herdbeast, and plants, food, weapons, and dozens of other small details.

Here's Orson Scott Card, author of *Ender's Game*, describing the challenge of building a realistic world: "There are two things. One is to make the world come alive and the other is to make it feel alive to the reader. And they are really two different things." The secret, Card suggests, is in the small things. "You need plenty of realistic detail that absolutely feels true . . . if you also have a lot of common everyday things going on, it helps."

The world you create—whether populated by talking cats or cyborgs—must have its own rules. Charles de Lint, author of *Svaha*, says that "There has to be boundaries and rules, and you don't go over them. And give them as much reality as possible."

Jane Yolen, author of *White Jenna* and *Dove Isabeau*, says it's important that "The author has played fair. The rules work as surely as gravity works in our world."

The next exercise is actual world-building. You'll create a world—the physical planet, the people, the cities, the technology, and the society. It may be a world that you'll use for a story or a novel, or simply a practice exercise that you'll discard while you move on to other creations.

Everything that follows may not be needed for every story or novel. And some areas will certainly need much more development. A heavily political novel set in an alien world will require more thought about the various political systems, not to mention the history of the planet. If you set your story on contemporary Earth, that familiar world will have to be less *created* than re-searched—except for those areas that are affected by the fantastic aspects of your plot.

I'll ask you questions to help you describe your world, and I will follow it with descriptions of a sample world that I created.

Feel free to go back and change different aspects of your world as you uncover secrets about it.

Exercise 2—World-Building

1—*The Planet . . .*

Stop, and picture a planet. Perhaps it's a clone of Earth, a medium-sized, blue-green planet of water and land. Or is it larger, perhaps a giant planet, with numerous moons? Or a smaller, almost tiny planet, where days and nights are separated by just hours? Be sure to think about the physical factors, such as gravity. As the planet's mass increases or decreases, so will the gravitational force change.

What kind of climate is found on the planet? Is it lined with temperate areas, or is it a hot, dry planet? Are there giant regions of frozen water threatening to cover the surface with icy glaciers?

What is it like internally? Do active volcanoes dot the surface, or are the mountains ancient and weathered? Is the planet covered with giant, dense jungles? Perhaps it resembles the planet from Ray Bradbury's marvelous *All Summer in a Day*, where it rains continuously.

Think of possible plants and animals that might be appropriate to the ecosystems found on the planet. What are the sources of food? What are the life cycles of the animals?

Make your decisions . . . and don't worry—you can go back and change your planet later.

Oceanus

Oceanus is a large, temperate planet, completely covered with water except for the two polar masses. Much of the sea area is shallow, often only a hundred feet deep. Yet there are also enormous pelagic valleys and canyons leading to black, abyssal trenches.

It was not always so. Thousands of years ago, something triggered the gradual warming that caused the great ice caps to shrink. And the ancient land of Oceanus, low and weathered, was claimed by the sea.

The planet is now banded by enormous currents and cross currents that wind their periodic way around the planet. Fierce, violent storms occur with a regularity that indicates they spring from the cyclical interaction of currents and wind systems.

There are four key ecosystems on the planet: the surface, the shallow sea, the mountainous ice caps, and the abyssal trenches. The surface contains the floating cities and a variety of exotic sea birds.

The shallow seas teem with life. The ice caps are considered a mysterious, unknown place . . . frozen and lifeless. The abyssal rifts and valleys harbor thermal vents that support strange and deadly life forms.

2—Sentient Creatures

In most cases you will want an intelligent life form in your world, unless the world is to serve as a common meeting ground for other groups—and then their worlds will need detailing, too.

If you write about Earth, you may be dealing with humans who are essentially the same as those who inhabit the planet today. But social, historical, and cultural factors may make their behavior and society very different. For example, in my novel, *Time of the Fox*, the *glasnost* era has led to a resurgence of KGB hardliners who are using time travel to change history and make hard-line Communism work. The world is similar to our own, but it is more vulnerable—unprepared for the vicious time attack.

The conflict in your story can also be enriched by having a number of creatures that are in opposition to each other. Silverberg's Majipoor featured six very different races of creatures. The planet was ripe with intrigue. On the other hand, Robert Heinlein's Martian from *Stranger in a Strange Land*, Michael Valentine Smith, was actually an Earth-born human, reared on Mars.

If you do create intelligent creatures, decide what they look like, and what they might resemble from the known world. In my novel, *The Wizard of Tizare*, there were two groups of intelligent creatures, the cat-like Mrem and the lizard-like Lishkash. The hostility between these two groups, a natural development for such different creatures, was built-in. It was fur versus scales, warm blood versus cold. They were the bitterest of enemies, fighting over their planet.

In many cases, you'll feel most comfortable making human-like creatures the central focus of your world. And that's fine, as long as you make sure that their life-style reflects the nature of your planet.

If your planet is largely a hot, tropical jungle, then shelter may not be a priority, and food might be in abundance. A planet in the throes of glaciers and an ice age would force completely different priorities on its residents.

If you opt for creatures of a more novel design—bird-like animals, intelligent dinosaurs, semi-simians . . . follow that nature through to its conclusion. My female cat-like Mrem were randy animals, modeled on the howling tabbies who haunt earthly backyards and alleyways. Preening was important to these intelligent creatures, as well as the markings of their fur.

Envision your creatures—and then follow that design to its logical conclusion.

The Intelligent Creatures of Oceanus— The Faah and the Delvin

The Faah are the humanoid survivors of the land-dwellers. With a technology and a culture reminiscent of the Earth's doomed Atlanteans, various Faah groups—

27

intelligent and resourceful—were able to prepare for the flooding.

A few Faah societies tried to survive in great ships. But most cooperated and organized the construction of giant floating cities. Later, those who survived in their ships were soon forced to seek shelter in the cities.

The Faah were eventually forced to trade with the feared Delvin, the communal creatures that lived in the sea. In some cases, there was conflict where the Faah tried to simply take what they wanted, like the coal-like coral that was used for fuel. A few Faah survived by living as pirates and preying on the cities.

Occasionally, a Faah can be blessed with a special ability, a psychic power that is found embarrassing in the more sophisticated cities. These special Faah are gifted with premonitions and the ability to see events to come. It is rumored that a few have been able to take this power further, to a black sea magic . . . which is why those "blessed" are sometimes shunned.

The Delvin are intelligent sea creatures, with limbs and three-fingered hands that give them the ability to make and use tools. They can, if they wish, communicate with each other telepathically, a factor not known by the Faah. They can emerge from the water with the help of a conch-like animal that can hold up to their gills.

The society of the Delvin had been peaceful, without stress or conflict, before the coming of the floating cities. But for over a thousand years they have become more and more involved in the trade and life of the surface-dwellers, often with unfortunate and violent results.

There are now extremist groups of Delvin who preach the extermination of the surface dwellers.

3—The History

Now, with a planet and an intelligent life form(s), it's time to create the history. Again, what has happened on your world will largely be shaped by the physical nature of the planet and by any inherent rivalries between competing life forms.

Have there been major wars on the planet? If so, what have they been about? What matters have been resolved, and what left unresolved, to fester . . .

Decide the major accomplishments of your intelligent life forms. List technological breakthroughs as well as high lights of exploration. Consider how population centers or cities were created. What political movements took hold, and how did they affect the life of the creatures?

What kind of government (or governments) is in place—and don't be afraid to be inventive. You can have any combination of anarchy and dictatorship, democracy and strict Communism. But no matter what systems you put in place, remember that you should have—in your background at least—a historical basis for them.

This history will probably grow and develop as you work on your world but—for now—try to quickly sketch in some high points that stick out.

What are the goals, the dreams of the dwellers on your planet . . . how have they been frustrated . . . and what will they do about it in the future?

Oceanus' History

Oceanus surface dwellers were forced to live on giant floating cities by the climactic changes that turned the planet into a giant sea world. The cities were constructed from the planet's plentiful native wood.

Each city was built in a way that resembles a floating Venice, with waterways passing through the city, and foot bridges. Weight and water displacement were a primary consideration, and they remain a concern even as the cities expand.

Most of the floating cities feature ancient, older sections surrounded by newer sections built from the tough sea wood, a strong, light-weight algae harvested by the Delvin in exchange for manufactured goods such as woven cloth and metal.

The smallest cities simply float on the great currents, harvesting the plentiful sea life and growing food in giant sea gardens. But others use giant sea sails that fill the city and enable them to change currents, controlling their food supply and avoiding the devastating sea storms and the dreaded cold regions.

And still other floating cities developed primitive engines that burn the fossil fuel mined by the Delvin. These mobile city-states are the most powerful, but they are the most vulnerable—dependent on the whims of the erratic Delvin.

As the floating city-states have grown, so has their own vision of their destiny and their role on Oceanus. Numerous small conflicts and wars have raged between the city-states, who launch invasions of swift fleets accompanied by armies of gliders.

But no major war, no giant conflict over the destiny of the planet, has—until now—broken out. But as the technology of the Faah advances, as the ambition and resentment of the Delvin is kindled, as the city-states compete for the underwater resources of the planet, war has become inevitable.

4—Religion and Magic

As important as political systems can be to your world, religion offers an important clue to the forces that drive a people—even when they are giant cats.

The belief systems on your world will often have their root in the world's history. To a great extent they are intertwined. But religion can also be a spur to tremendous ideological conflict that can be played out on the battlefield. Determining the belief systems on your planet can be key to driving your plot.

There are the alternatives of pantheism, monotheism, deism, and even atheism. Is there one religion in your world, or many? To what extent do the religions promote fanaticism?

You are free to give your planet's religious systems as strange a supernatural spin as you wish. But the belief systems should be tied to both the environment, the history, and the nature of your creatures.

If your SF tale will have more fantasy elements and less

science, you may want to create a full-blown magic system. Anything is possible—just as long as you make everything coherent, with the rules clearly spelled out as to who can do what and why.

Heinlein's Michael Valentine Smith was gifted with certain paranormal powers, including the ability to "discorporate" people into another dimension. The wizards in my book, *The Wizard of Tizare*, were able to see visions of the future. It's been said that magic is simply science that we don't understand. It can be powerful, but it must always have limits.

The Religion and Magic of Oceanus

The different Faah societies have a variety of religions, from a primitive pantheism to a near Judeo-Christian monotheism. There have been prophets, and—in one case—a historical savior. But there is also a growing cult belief in something that is the source of the "sea magic."

The Delvin worship a single deity, a being from the deep that supposedly resides at the center of the planet. It is this being, they say, who controls the life of the planet. It is not a benevolent deity. The Delvin fear the volcanic openings at the hydrothermal vents and the strange life rumored to be found there as signs of the fierce nature of this "God."

4—Culture

The cultural background of your world gives a depth to the creatures who inhabit it. There may be unique art forms which should be related to the nature of your creatures.

Literature and studying could be highly prized—or again, they may be looked upon as grievous activities. The art forms of your world could be very similar to earthly ones—such as dancing, singing, painting, etc. Silverberg's Majipoor had entertainment cubes with a vast library that could be accessed. The cat-like Mrem highly prized dancing.

Create novel art forms to reflect *your* creatures' deepest yearnings. Snake-like creatures may have made the coiling of their bodies into a subtle artistic ritual, filled with importance.

Don't expect to create all the forms of art and entertainment in your world. Just try to establish some general guidelines and examples which seem to follow from the nature of your intelligent creatures and their planet.

The Culture of Oceanus

At the time of the flooding, the Faah were developing a rich cultural heritage, with a tradition of philosophical inquiry. An aesthetic appreciation was the foundation of many of the societies.

This has—to some extent—continued for the thousands of years of the floating cities. But the enforced insularity, the need for cooperation and the rules governing the tenuous society, has turned many of the larger city-states into tyrannies ruled by autocrats who act in a capricious and sometimes cruel manner.

Thus, though the largest city-states see themselves as

enlightened—in the fashion of the Renaissance—there is a brutality that runs through much of the society.

Still—painting, music and dance abound . . . especially painting and the visual arts, where the power of the beautiful image is treated with an almost religious veneration. Those gifted with an artistic talent are considered special. The Image-makers are treated as the most-esteemed members of the society, since the world of the Faah has such definite limits.

Great art competitions are held, with rewards and honors. Some impute a special ability to those who create images with an aesthetic power.

5—Science

Science on your world may have led to similar breakthroughs found in Earth's scientific history—or completely different developments may have taken place.

Sometimes, religious beliefs will interact—usually negatively—with scientific knowledge. The important thing to think about is what *needs* will drive the scientific studies and the technological breakthroughs of your world?

If the planet is cold, then heating and shelter will be areas of concern. If the planet is overcrowded and its creatures underfed, then production, exploration, and perhaps even interplanetary travel will be the goals. A jungle environment could lead to deadly diseases, making medicine important.

War always drives technological development, providing spin-off benefits to the society, but also creating ever-more efficient killing systems.

Again, don't expect to list here all the scientific developments that have occurred on the planet. Instead, deal with the key problems that technology would attack. Later, you can add new insights as you write about the characters on your planet.

The Science of Oceanus

The technology of the Faah has not progressed much since the flooding. Some city-states have engines, while others do not because they cannot gather the necessary resources. Weapons of choice remain the sword and the crossbow, though there are small rifles that fire—often ineffectively. A weak gunpowder is very rare.

Research is geared to one goal—a way for the Faah to live, for some period at least, under the water. The Delvin have a conch-like animal that, when placed to their gills, lets them emerge out from the water for a short period of time.

They can speak the language of the Faah with a guttural sound ridiculed by the surface-dwellers. The Faah enjoy no such advantage. It is the goal of all their science.

Other scientists work to understand the pattern of the violent storms that can destroy even the larger cities. Strange biological and metaphysical experiments are undertaken, similar to the experiments of mediaeval alchemy, to help the Faah to become more closely aligned with the sea.

6—Tying It All Together

You should have, by now, sketched out ideas for a world that includes physical features, intelligent creatures, religion, science, and culture. Not all those ideas will be needed when you set a story on a world. Some information may stay as background, while other material may be discarded when it simply does not fit into your final conception.

To finish, try writing a three- or four-paragraph description of your world now, *without* looking at your notes. Write an overview, a short description of your world.

See if you can now tie the key factors together—how physical features affected the history . . . the way the history spurred religion . . . what the technology has done to the environment . . . the way the culture has reflected the struggle.

Imagine all the components coming together—and then write it down.

An Overview of Oceanus

Oceanus is an immense water planet. While there are two giant, mysterious ice masses located at the north and south poles of the planet, it is unknown whether there is any land underneath the mile-high ice.

Sprawling floating cities—the result of millennia of construction and reconstruction—float on the tremendous currents of the planet. A few of these city-states

have batteries of engines fed by a submerged fossil fuel—
a coal-like rock. Other, smaller cities can hoist gigantic
sails that fly from every part of the city. But most simply
drift, following the seasonal pattern of the currents.

All these cities are filled with the romance and intrigue of Venice during the Renaissance. . . . The Faah
struggle on their floating cities while, below them, the
Delvin grow impatient to rule the sea lanes.

One floating city, Kilt, is the primary focus. The
Aman, Kilt's hereditary ruler, struggles for planetary
dominance. Other floating cities plot behind the scenes,
as the tentative peace of the planet is about to be shat-
tered.

Stories about your world should already be occurring to
you, drawn simply from the nature of the physical and
historical forces on your planet. Perhaps characters are
appearing, ready to populate your world, with their own
involved personal history and background.

But before focusing on the characters who will be the
most important part of your story, it's time to do the
research to make sure that the fantastic world that you've
created has as much reality in it as possible.

CHAPTER
4

Making It Real

Here's how I learned about drowning . . . what exactly happens when someone, for one reason or another, is stuck underwater and has to breathe H_2O.

I was autographing my then-current book, *Beneath Still Waters* (1989), at a convention in Colorado. A young man came up to my table, with long black hair and the look of someone hoping to make it as a lead singer in a heavy metal band.

He told me his name, I signed the book, and he took it. And then he said, "So . . . a lot of this takes place underwater?"

"Yes . . . there's a lot of diving scenes."

He smiled, and then he told me that he was a diver. Not only that, he said that he was a diving consultant, leading underwater tours, training people, and doing commercial diving. Serious stuff.

"Great," I said. "Maybe you'll have some comments after you read the book." He seemed enthused and we exchanged cards.

And, in about a week, I received a hefty packet from Colorado. It was from my new diver friend. He enjoyed the book, he said, but . . .

Then for five double-sided pages he proceeded to educate me about diving, including extreme cold-water diving—which is in my book; dives into toxin-contaminated water, deep water dives, and, to be sure, drowning . . . how the throat closes to prevent water from entering until the lungs, starved for oxygen, force the water to gush in.

My research for that book had been good, but not quite good enough for a pro. For a reader like that, my book lost credibility. And worse—I missed out on some absolutely terrific background and information that would have been wonderful in my book.

It was a good lesson in the importance of making my fiction real . . . not only to avoid dumb mistakes, but to make my world stronger and more exciting.

Here are some techniques for making your SF world as real as possible.

Recognize Your Expertise

Whatever your life is like, you are an expert on that kind of life, whether it's living in the mountains of Alaska or the streets of San Jose. From the humid south, to the frigid north, each one of us has a bit of the "real world" that we know a hell of a lot better than millions of people.

And there's not only geography, but there are also the

people you know—your family, your friends, your acquaintances, your enemies . . . they make up a pool of personalities that can feed the creation of your fictional characters.

Some of these people may be excellent resources. A cousin who's a policeman can tell you about handling firearms. A friend who's a weekend sailor can show you what it means to tack and come about, so you can bring a real experience to your writing about giant ships on a water planet.

In my book *Hour of the Scorpion* (1991), northern New York City has been leveled, including Columbia University—site of the novel's Time Lab. My attendance of Columbia University's Graduate School helped me recreate the Morningside Heights area—even with all the buildings gone . . .

Do Some *Real* Research

We all know what it's like to hunker down in a library seat and plod through ancient, out-of-date tomes searching for facts.

But that won't give your book the depth that it needs. If you're going to try to bring an alien world to life, or a vision of a future earth, you have to get to sources that match your vision.

Some fine source books may be found in the library—on everything from terraforming to genetic manipulation. But you can also phone institutions and groups to ask the specific questions for which you need answers, whether it's the location of the biggest particle accelerator in the world, or the name of the deepest abyss in the Pacific.

While working on *WURM*, a novel with scenes near the hydrothermal vents of the Atlantic, I called Marie Tharp—who, with Bruce Heezen, created the first ocean floor map and discovered the Mid-Atlantic Ridge.

I called Tharp to ask a question about the ridge and about her discovery of the underwater mountain range. But we also talked about the strange hydrothermal vents. Our talk brought me information and inspiration that fueled a number of key scenes in the book.

Letters can also bring a cornucopia of information. I sent a short query about submersibles to the Woods Hole Oceanographic Institution, and it brought me a deluge of slides, background information, and booklets which allowed me to take my book even further into the techno-fiction realm.

Computer Information Services, such as GEnie and CompuServe, offer extensive libraries and data bases that can save trips to the library. All you need is a computer and a modem, and you can search for your specific topic and let the information service call up the appropriate documents.

Always keep your eye open for items that have potential value to future research. At a book convention, I saw a display of intriguing new maps from a company called Van Dam. These incredible maps unfold to give detailed, bird's-eye views of everything from the moon, Mars, and the ocean, to major cities like New York and San Francisco. When *Hour of the Scorpion* took my time-traveling hero to San Francisco, the Van Dam map helped me plot my character's movements.

But what if you don't know an institution or group to contact for your topic?

Start by thinking about your topic and try to get one word to describe it. Then check the Yellow and White Pages for any group or organization that might seem relevant. Often a small group will lead you to a larger, very helpful one. Is there a society devoted to robotics? Start with a technical school, perhaps with its librarian. Or try calling a science museum.

And if you do go to the library, even out-of-date reference books will often have a bibliography listing groups, clubs, and associations concerned with your topic. Most libraries also offer an inter-library loan system and can get any current book from a larger system.

Go the Extra Mile

File this under the heading "field trips."

You should hit the road and see people and places, up close and personal. Get out and experience what you're writing about—or as close to it as you can. Do it with all your sensory switches on, ready to soak in the whole experience.

After I saw the background material that the Woods

Hole Oceanographic Institution sent me, I knew I just *had* to go there. I drove to Cape Cod and studied the buildings and layout of the place, all of which I used in *WURM*. I also got to see the research vessel and submersibles up close.

Sometimes you can get a special tour, using your writing project as a calling card.

I was writing about Atlantic City and gambling, and the Press Department of Trump's Taj Mahal not only arranged a stay at the hotel but a special behind-the-scenes look at how a casino is run. I saw things that only the casino employees normally see, and that kind of background is hard to come by through ordinary research.

But going the extra mile doesn't always involve making special arrangements or plunging into icy lakes in early spring.

Before I started writing about Coney Island (soon to be infected by the strange hydrothermal creatures of *WURM*), I spent a blustery winter's day walking the splintered boardwalk, avoiding the homeless figures that stumbled towards me eager for spare change.

The rides were all bundled up with tarps, sleeping until the summer sun would awaken them. The few businesses open were doing a brisk business—Nathan's Famous was selling its top-drawer hot dogs, the sweet-smelling fudge place had a fresh batch for sale, and the carousel, open year-round, was singing its thumping, jangly song.

Even if a scene you're writing involves something as simple as a mountainside ramble—on Earth or on Jupiter's moon Io—you can make an effort to get the "feel" of it right. Visit your local outfitter for a pair of climbing boots and hit the mountain trails.

Here are a few guidelines to help you capture real-life experiences when you're on the road.

- *Bring a notebook.* You'll learn more from your mountain hike or a behind-the-scenes tour of the Columbia University Robotics Lab if you take notes. Jot down your impressions, feelings, even character descriptions. Note the sounds and smells of the place. Let yourself wax poetic if it will help you capture the experience.

- *Carry a microcassette recorder.* Of course, you can record your observations directly on the recorder. But you can also capture the *sounds* of a place. And if you get a chance to talk with someone—your diving instructor, a pit boss at the blackjack tables, a research physicist for IBM—you're ready for an impromptu interview.

- *Travel with a camera.* It should have a zoom lens, so that you can get shots at a distance. Later, you can decorate your office or work station with photos of submersibles, the view from Mt. Kahtahdin, or sunset at the Everglades. The photos will help bring your mind back to that place, to that time, so that you can nail it down for your reader.

• *Do a post-mortem.* When the experience is over—
and you're back home—sit down and write down your
impressions. (Regular journal keeping should be part
of your writing discipline.) Write questions to yourself
. . . why people acted in certain ways, why things
worked the way they do. Try to recall the telling details
of an experience.

At Coney Island, I passed by the closed Astroland,
walking on the cracked sidewalk. And I saw a dead dog, a
mutt, curled up close against the wire mesh fence.

I kept walking. But later, I remembered the shock of
seeing it there. And I wrote down questions . . . How did
it die? And why the hell hadn't anyone come by to remove
it? Just how abandoned *is* Coney Island?

Dissect your experience. Not only what you saw and
heard and smelled, but what it all means . . .

• *Expand your library.* A good encyclopedia and a
phone directory will get you far, but there are other
sources which should be close at hand.

Get a top-notch atlas, something on a par with *Goode's
World Atlas*, which not only has geographical maps, but
also shows climate, terrain, and population. The Mich-
elin series of Guide Books are essential for any writer
with a story set in Europe. Star maps can help you locate
your world in space—and give you an eerie idea of just
how far away your world may be. Vintage Books has a
nifty book, *The Map Catalog*, filled with every kind of

map and chart on the earth—and off it—that you can order.

Find the specialized reference books that give you real depth in your area. For my Time Warrior series, I used over a dozen books on World War II, including the massive *Illustrated History of World War II* from Portland House. For an inside look at how everyday things work, you must have a copy of David Macaulay's *The Way Things Work* (Houghton-Mifflin). For the names of such items as the thing you pick up when the phone rings (it's called the "handset," by the way) get *What's What*, published by Ballantine.

Joe R. Lansdale, author of *The Drive-In* and *Cold in July*, had this to say about the value of real experiences: "Even a simple fist fight is different if you've been in one and you're writing about it. I used to teach martial arts, and I used to box . . . and they have a fever about them."

This is a fever that will be hard to imagine without sampling those experiences. Take road trips, record your experiences, get some good maps, and your imagination should be able to do the rest . . .

Beyond Research

Sitting alone in your room, office, wherever you write, working on a science fiction epic or a fantastic story of post-Armageddon Earth can distance you from the reality that you need.

It's hard to imagine 50-below-zero temperatures and freezing winds when it's 95+ degrees and the sun is out for a godawful 15 hours a day. What can you do to help your imagination create a much chillier reality?

You can surround yourself with bits and pieces of reality, images and objects to inspire and stimulate you, and to keep you focused on the way things are in your fictional world.

Try gathering mementos, artifacts, newspaper clippings . . . bits of cultural flotsam and jetsam to give you a feeling of a "place" or the "experience."

A match book from Stan and Mary's Restaurant in Key Largo—where they serve the best conch chowder in the Keys—can bring the restaurant, its bar, and the local characters back to life for me.

Photographs of giant Antarctic bergs floating in ice-blue water may take some of the heat away. A program from the old Fillmore, with psychedelic lettering announcing The Byrds, made the late sixties a lot closer when my hero jumped back in time.

If your doctor forbids mountain climbing, invest in a good climbing hammer anyway. Just hefting the heavy metal hammer will give you a feel for what it must be like to tackle the Grand Tetons.

Think of your settings, and then collect images that are closely identified with those locations. Film Director Alfred Hitchcock always used what most clearly symbolized the locations of his suspense films. So New York became the Statue of Liberty in *Saboteur*, and South Dakota was

Mt. Rushmore in *North by Northwest*, and we knew we were in Holland from the white windmills of *Foreign Correspondent*.

The rain-drenched planet of Ray Bradbury's story "All Summer in A Day" has only one major detail that hammers home its "alien-ness"—the non-stop rain, interrupted by only the briefest few minutes of sunshine once every seven years. We never lose sight of the oppressiveness of that one detail.

For period pieces, fill your walls with photocopies of newspaper headlines from the year you're writing about, and dozens of old photos from books and magazines.

My office is currently littered with pictures of ants and charts on their genetic information, as well as maps of Westchester—all key elements in a new novel I'm working on. Months ago, a lost Brooklyn filled my office walls, with photos of Steeplechase Park—demolished in 1965—and the Farragut Pool, where I swam during the summers. There were also maps of the old ferry routes, and photos of restaurants; I surrounded myself with that vanished world.

Going beyond the mere *words* of research to actual objects and images can help keep your story alive for you.

Fill Your Senses

When I was writing *Hour of the Snake*, I played the juke box hits of the Vietnam era. Most of the music was corny and insipid, especially when compared with the album rock being released. But it was this music that the G.I.s heard on Armed Forces radio and in the honky-tonk bars.

For another book, I started jogging in a nearby nature preserve, padding through the thick trees and bushes, hearing the crunch of dry leaves, the snap of pants catching at my feet. And I used those impressions to imagine what it must have been like for a character who *had* to escape, running through a wilderness, while someone . . . or something gained on him.

Before I started *WURM*, I walked the winter beach, letting the sounds and sensations make indelible impressions.

Advice from Writers Who Make It Real

Charles de Lint, author of *Svaha* and *Drinking Down the Moon*, says that, "There has to be boundaries and rules for your world, and you don't go over them. And give them as much reality as possible. . . . Research is an important and ongoing process. I did an incredible amount of research on Gypsies for a recent book."

Jane Yolen, author of *White Jenna* and *Dove Isabeau*, says it's important that, "The author has played fair. The rules work as surely as gravity works in our world. When I was writing about dragons, I wanted to be sure dragons could fly. I wasn't going to do a fairy-tale dragon. So I researched into large birds, hollow bones, and the effects of various wings. . . ."

Joe R. Lansdale, author of the science-fiction/fantasy

novels *The Drive In* and *The Drive-In II*, as well as editor of the western/horror collection *Razored Saddles*, was born in East Texas in 1951. And both that place and time are important in bringing reality to his work.

"There are no trees, no lakes in East Texas . . . it's different from the rest of Texas. I came of age in the sixties—a time of social unrest, but I remember the fifties."

This background fills Lansdale's work, as does his family. "My grandmother remembered covered wagons, and my father grew up with relatives that fought the Civil War. My dad couldn't read or write . . . and he used to travel from one country fair to another, fighting for money. He had incredible stories . . . and they're all in my head."

Joe affirms the old saw, "Write What You Know." "I love Drive-Ins" . . . hence his book. His award-winning story, "The Night They Closed the Horror Show" was based on reality. "Everything happened," Joe said . . . "not all in one night, but it all happened. . . ."

Exercise 3

Take the world that you created in Chapter Four and write a two-to-three-paragraph scene set on that world. Use some real-life experience that you've had, perhaps an encounter with an unusual character, or the time your car died on a snowy road. Transform your real life into a moment on your fictional world.

Part 2:

CREATING CHARACTERS

CHAPTER
5

Creating Realistic Characters
. . . Even When They're Not
Human

You have a world, and you've done everything to make it as real as possible. What's missing now?

Any book or story will live or die based on its characters, but that's even more true for science fiction and fantasy. As soon as you're dealing with themes and worlds beyond the normal reality, you're fighting a natural incredulity on the part of the reader.

And your characters will have to be as real as you can make them.

We all start with one very real limitation. There is only one character that we know completely, and that is ourselves. Everyone else is perceived through their public and private mask. We only guess at their motivations, and their deep goals—their secret drives and problems. The true nature, the internal workings, of the people we *know* remains a matter of speculation.

And even in the case of our own psyche, there are black holes that don't let us see everything that drives us. Perhaps one reason that so many successful writers and film-makers go into therapy, as soon as they can afford it, is to get a better grasp of the central character in their life—themselves.

But the basic rules for creating strong characters in SF aren't any different from those for any other storytelling. There are added concerns and problems raised by working with SF material—which we'll deal with in the next chapter—but first we'll look at some general guidelines for creating characters.

Point of View

There have been only three times in my writing career when I received direct, relevant help that changed my writing.

Once was when famed author Harlan Ellison phoned me to offer a quick analysis of some early chapters of a book I had finished. Harlan referred me to some key essays on science fiction—information I'll pass on to you in the appendix to this book.

But the most important incident occurred when I was searching for a reputable agent shortly after my first book had been published. I was carrying around the initial chapters of a brand new book and showing them to prospective agents.

One top agent read my material and offered to meet with me—even though she admitted she didn't have the time or space to take me on as a client.

I wasn't, at that point, pulling down too much money

with my novels, and as a client would have been a big loss leader. Still, the agent saw some potential and wanted to meet with me.

And believe me, what happened next has got to be a rare experience. It just doesn't happen like this.

I sat down in the agent's office in a beautiful brownstone building. She had gone through the first chapters of my book, filling my pages with marks and questions.

Some of the points she raised were the simple kinds of problems I probably would have fixed when I started to revise the chapters. But she raised one point that was key, vital to making my story work.

"Who are your main characters?" she asked.

I told her, rattling off half a dozen characters' names. And she shook her head.

"No, that's way too many. Have three, maybe four main characters—tops—and then you must write the story completely from their point of view. . . ."

She pushed my pages to me, showing a section where two boys, Bill and Jackie, were taking a last walk through their old town—about to be buried beneath a lake to make way for a dam.

"See, here," she said. "First, we're seeing everything through Bill's eyes and then—in the same section—you shift to Jackie's point of view. The reader gets yanked away from the character, and then back again."

I nodded. I didn't need her to say any more. Of course . . . I could see that I let my point of view float around, first in one character, then in another, now in nobody.

And there was more . . .

She pointed to a line where one of the boys passes by the old five-and-dime store. "Let the character respond to the place," she said, "from *his* point of view. Let him think about the waitress behind the counter who always gave him a free refill of Cokes. Let him remember the heavenly smells of the candy counter. Get inside his head, and experience the walk through his eyes. . . ."

And—as they say—I *heard* what she was saying. To some extent, I had been doing what she advised instinctively. But I had been erratic, and I'd let the point of view shift without being aware of it.

Now, there are writing courses that tell you the omniscient author—the third-person, objective—point of view is just fine. In that style, the author is almost another character, watching the action in the story and commenting on it.

Jerry Pournelle and Larry Niven's massive book *Lucifer's Hammer* required a third-person viewpoint to tell a story of impending disaster from space. With that kind of epic scope, an omniscient author was needed.

And there are, of course, many cases of short stories, and even successful novels, written in the first person (using the infamous "I"). Jay McInerney's *Bright Lights, Big City* is a good, best-selling example.

But while the third-person objective point of view knows too much, the first-person point of view is usually much too limiting.

To make your characters real, limit your main point of view characters to three or four. Root *everything* you write in the character who is the focal point for that chapter or section. We'll look at an example of this in the next chapter.

Make Your Characters React

Your characters have to enter a scene with their "switches" on, ready to react to everything that happens to them. These reactions won't always be physical. Often, it will simply be a painful or sweet memory that an event triggers in a character. Maybe some thoughts, some concerns are aroused by a chain of events.

To make this work, you'll have to try to write a scene while you envision yourself *experiencing* it as that character. Instead of thinking "What does that *character* observe?" better to think: "What do *I* observe?" We *see* lots of things, but only a few elements in our immediate environment stand out as having importance or meaning.

Follow significant lines of reverie, not every meandering thought of a character. A hair ribbon on the ground might summon, for a character, thoughts of a young daughter lost to a strange disease. The way her hair shined under the artificial sunlight . . . the sound of the girl's laughter echoing down the corridors of an underground space colony.

You can't let every object experience or encounter trigger a string of memories or thoughts. But—used judiciously—such reactions become absolutely vital to making your character stunningly real.

Give Your Characters Goals

An important thing to remember, when you try to get into the mind of your point of view characters, is that they are not *you*.

Not only will your characters have different personalities, but their *goals* will, in most cases, be vastly different. Your goal is to write a story, or a novel. You want to be accepted as a writer, as a creative artist.

Your character's long-range goals might include escaping something that happened to them in the past, or running from the guilt of a bad decision. Or a character could be searching for respect from his or her peers. They could be fighting the ignorance of scientists or society. They could want something—an achievement, some breakthrough—more than anything else, no matter what the cost.

Characters will also have short-term goals, just as you do. You may want to finish a chapter before going to bed for the night. A character may want to find some food on a barren planet, or she may want to escape the armed security cyborgs that are looking for her.

Goals—the large ones and the small ones—go a long way towards defining who your character is, and what motivates them. They affect the decisions the character makes. Before you write one sentence about a character, you should have clear ideas about what he or she wants.

Not that you have to give it to them in the book. In fact, you can have a lot of fun keeping the character frustrated. This can act like an engine, driving the book.

In my first time travel novel, *Time of the Fox*, Jim Tiber wants to study the Beatles during their time in Hamburg, well before their success. He hopes that some on-site time travel work will help him get his thesis approved.

This goal leads him to break into Columbia University's secret Red Building and take some unauthorized time travel. Jim gets to meet the Beatles—briefly—before getting sucked into a war being fought in the past by forces from the future.

Jim's goals then change, as he wants to get back to his own time. But he finds himself trapped into helping the time lab get history back to normal—actions that put him and his lover, Alessandra, at risk.

And that's another important fact to remember.

Short-term goals may change, as contingencies force changes for characters. But the characters' underlying goals should stay relatively steady in the course of the story.

Give Your Characters Lots of Problems

Nobody likes problems. But problems—and the conflict they bring—makes life undeniably interesting for your character. Sometimes beginning authors tend to want to smooth the way for characters, having them resolve thorny difficulties much too easily.

Actually, you should be doing just the opposite. Once readers know and care about a person, they will be pulling for them to succeed. If you add problems that interfere with a character's goals, you will be adding tension and suspense. The more you keep your main actors on the ropes, the more suspense and tension you create for the readers.

Your job, plain and simple, is to make life difficult for your characters. Have your hero fumble the key to the locked security gate . . . and then let it fall down an open grate. Have your heroine rescue someone only to find themselves hopelessly trapped.

The problems you throw at your characters should not only be external ones. There should be inner conflicts, such as guilt or fear or panic, or a host of personal stumbling blocks that will make the story tense, the personality interesting, and the suspense delicious.

Dean R. Koontz's genre-spanning novels, mixing SF, horror, and mystery, often feature characters who have problems that they're working out, both internally and externally. In Koontz's *Midnight*, a key character is disabled and confined to a wheelchair. This makes the danger that person faces all the more thrilling, and his struggle more heroic.

At the end of your story or novel, of course, you'll want to resolve most of the conflicts you've created. That is, after all, the point of the story. But there may still be some dangling threads, letting the story continue to play out in the reader's mind.

Give Us a Hero

. . . Or even an antihero. This applies most strongly to novels, where you want the reader to return to the book, day after day. There must be a character that engages our emotions and intellect, someone that becomes the central figure and the protagonist of your story.

The protagonist should be a character that we know better than any of the other actors in the story. It will be someone whose goals readers can root for, whose problems readers want to see solved.

Since you'll want the reader to empathize with this character, it should be someone we can like. This person shouldn't be obnoxious, vapid, irritating, egocentric, malicious, wimpy, pathetic—well, you get the idea.

On the other hand, this central point of view character—your hero or heroine—can't be perfect. Perfect people aren't very real, and—besides—who cares about a perfect person? So your basically sympathetic character has to have some personality problems, idiosyncrasies, and hang-ups that let the reader know that this person is human.

A fear of heights, an insecurity with women, a cavalier attitude towards duty and responsibility, a taste for gambling or psycho-active chemicals, can all make this main character, your protagonist, more engaging.

Maybe he/she has a temper, or a violent streak. It will be most interesting if the protagonist's flaws dovetail in interesting ways with the conflicts to be resolved. When

61

these flaws become part of the forces arrayed against the character—forces which can include the environment itself—you have a rich basis for a multi-level story that can engage its readers.

Write Biographies

Your characters had lives before the story began, and you need to document that life. Record all the mundane facts, all the vitae of your characters, including the date of birth, height, weight, and hair and eye color. Go into education and work experience, as well as family background.

Invent other events in the character's life, things that shaped the goals or problems of the character. Include childhood accidents, family dysfunctions, and tragedy. Do a sketch of the character, or try to imagine what person you know, perhaps an actor from film or TV, that they most resemble.

Try to give characters life before you make them live on your pages.

Do What Your Characters Do

If your characters are skin-divers or rocket scientists or champion chess players, learn how to do what they do. You may not reach their level of proficiency, but you'll gain a real understanding of what makes them tick. For my novel *Beneath Still Waters*, I went to a dive shop to learn about underwater microphones. Later I climbed on top of a dam . . . just what my characters had to do.

Following the above guidelines can lead any writer of fiction to create strong characters. But what of the special requirements of science fiction and fantasy? Don't they have special rules that govern the characters in a speculative universe?

Yes—and no. The basic rules of characterization remain the same. But there are special requirements that you'll have to deal with, depending on your story, its theme, and its scope. Next, we'll look at some SF characters in detail to see how those differences can make the job of creating characters more difficult—and also a lot more interesting . . .

Exercise

Look back at your world and write a biography for a character who inhabits that world. Tie some of the goals and problems of the character to the limitations of the environment that you created. Include vital details about the character, but also try to make the character someone that you would like to know more about, and someone you'd like to write about.

CHAPTER
6

Characters in Science Fiction
and Fantasy

There are a number of obvious differences in characterization when you work in SF. If your characters are psy-
chologically confused robots or moody, bear-like aliens
with telepathic powers, there are important considera-
tions that you'd best keep in mind when you're writing
about them.

Your characters will have to reflect the environment,
the time, and the milieu of your world. Whatever the
global and cosmic concerns of that time and place, they
must somehow have an impact on your main characters. If
those personalities have a special nature or unusual abili-
ties, these factors will have to be integrated into their
character profile.

A common mistake with beginning writers in SF is to
make *too* much of an unusual aspect of a character.
("He brushed at his antennae, which always seemed to
get caught in the leafy branches of the wilbur
trees. . . .")

Remember that whatever the characteristic is that

you're emphasizing, it should appear normal and natural against the backdrop of the rest of the character's traits.

To see how this works, look at the following section from my novel, *Hour of the Scorpion*. To set the scene, Jim Tiber finds himself inside Jack McShane's mind in San Francisco circa 1968, surrounded by the turmoil of what was called—briefly—the counter-culture. McShane is a Vietnam lieutenant home on leave because his father is dying . . .

And then Tiber, from 1997, has to take McShane's place and hit the streets of late-sixties Haight-Ashbury to look for McShane's brother, Will—who has vanished into this world of acid rock and hippies.

Read the section, and then I'll discuss the special concerns about the character that I kept in mind while writing . . .

It could have been any poor, inner-city neighborhood.

Except—Jim thought—most ghettos aren't this colorful. The streets here were filled with kids, garish and clown-like in their fringed vests, broad-brimmed hats, and bell-bottomed jeans dotted with a quilt-like covering of patches.

And the shops—which were once a dry cleaners, or a neighborhood deli—had also undergone transformation.

Jim walked past an establishment called the "Light Fantastic." It was apparently doing a brisk business in posters and ultra-violet lights. There was a poster in the front window, bathed in purple light from a long bulb on each side. It showed a ship, some Rembrandt or Dürer rendering, sailing into a swirling red and blue spiral.

The UV light made the day-glo colors alive, the picture shimmering, almost 3-D.

Just the thing to study while turning on . . .

Another shop offered pipes and papers, essential weapons in the counter-culture revolution. A loudspeaker above the door was transmitting marching orders to the freak army. Jimi Hendrix thumped out the abrasive, kick-ass licks of Purple Haze.

Man, thought Jim, would Hendrix be freaked out to realize that the late nineties brought a host of Jimi impersonators gigging everywhere, from the money pits of Vegas to the Rainbow Room. Even the hippies became middle-aged.

He crossed another block, and then turned up to Ashbury . . . following it down to a street named Clayton. Someone hissed at him from a stoop.

"Hash, joints, bennies . . . Got what you're looking for, man." Jim looked at the guy sitting on the steps. He was balding. And though he had bell-bottoms and a goatee, the drug seller was about five years too late for this trip. More of a businessman, probably, dealing bad acid to the kids from Marin County who came into town to "blow their mind."

Jim shook his head. And again he felt that anger, that nasty feeling inside, a feeling as if he'd like to smash the guy. He's a predator. The first of the legion that would come to own the cities.

"Peace, man," the guy, the vulture man called to him from the steps.

"Screw you," Jim said back to him. Wishing—that the guy would say something back. (And knowing . . . this is McShane in charge. This isn't my thing. I'm about as non-confrontational as they come.)

He kept walking down Clayton, and he saw other residents of the Haight area. Old ladies pushing their small wagons filled with two bags of groceries. A bunch of black men stood around, talking, probably wondering where all the grinning, goofy-faced white kids came from.

And then he came to the building.

The sign said: The New Haight Health Collective and, in smaller letters . . . "All welcome."

Jim pulled open the door and walked in. He was in a waiting room. Some freaks sat on a couch. One kid, with hair tumbling below his shoulder, tapped his foot nervously. He banged at his knee. To his right, there was a big black woman with two little kids running around, hiding under the chairs. A girl in a big paisley dress— hiding what Jim guessed was a pregnancy—sat morosely by herself.

Later, Jim Tiber meets McShane's brother . . .

Jim stood outside, leaning against a "no parking" sign, the balmy winter sun on his neck. A cool breeze whipped up the street. It sent a scattering of lost newspaper pages scurrying around as if looking for a trash barrel.

A red car went by, a classic Mustang with brilliant white-walled tires. And when Jim turned back to the Medical Collective door, he saw his brother.

No, McShane's brother. . . . He had to tell himself that. Because looking at this lanky kid, pushing his long hair off his face, brought this incredible tidal wave of feelings.

He saw Will as a kid, with a crew cut, running after him, after McShane, wanting to go with him to the

67

movies. And McShane calling back to him to go home. You're too little, he yelled. You'll get scared by the monster, Will. *Real scared.*

And his kid brother would stop and McShane would take a quick glance before picking up his pace. Nobody wanted a little brother tagging along.

Now the kid, Will, was nearly a man standing here. What was he? Sixteen . . . Seventeen? Still my little brother. And Jim felt other feelings, undefined jealousies, and anger—

"Hey look," Will said, taking a step towards him. "I'm not going back home, can you dig that? I've got a place to crash, and I've got some good friends. I don't need my old man jumping on my case about my hair, or my music, and I sure as hell don't need you playing big brother."

What's going on here? Jim thought. What's the history, the years of buried garbage that I'm trying to deal with here? That I *can't* deal with . . .

Now, let's look at these sections and see what I did with the character of Jim Tiber, who is, temporarily, Jack McShane.

First, you can see that I kept to Jim's point-of-view throughout the two sections. We see the Haight-Ashbury area, the burgeoning world of hippies, through his 1997 eyes.

Jim sees the kids in their fringed vests and bell-bottoms. He thinks about Hendrix playing through the loudspeaker—old music that Jim Tiber had studied. When Jim has an encounter with a drug dealer, he sees him through the eyes of someone from a world that has been ravaged by drugs.

But—at the same time—Jim Tiber feels the presence of the person's mind he's borrowing. In my series, the time travellers enter the consciousness of other people. They coexist with that consciousness, but bits and pieces of that other person leak through.

So here, Jim feels an anger, an almost violent anger at the dealer.

And here is where the special needs of the book determine a different approach to character. There are, to some extent, *two* personalities here. And so Jim Tiber will feel the presence of another point of view inserting itself.

And—believe me—this can get confusing. I told you that the whole point is to stay rooted in *one* point of view; here, we can have *two* in one person. Likewise, there can be different goals, reactions, and emotions based on the extent that McShane's consciousness can be felt by Jim Tiber.

In the sections sampled here, this is most clearly seen where Jim has a memory—actually McShane's memory—of his little brother chasing after him. The point of view character has to have a double-reaction. He has to react to the memory itself, and also to the sheer fact that unwanted memories and feelings are popping up, confusing him.

Of course this "double-think" is a large part of the fun of dealing with time travel. In this case, there were some obvious steps I had to take to make the thing work.

First, I had to have Jim Tiber, time traveler, react to his unwanted emotions, feelings, and thoughts. They should bounce off him, creating confusing ripples of feeling. Because he reacts so strongly to the unwanted memories, the reader feels those reactions, and accepts the weird occurrence.

If Jim Tiber just had those thoughts pop up—and we didn't see him struggling with them—the whole situation would be unbelievable and fantastic. But Tiber does the doubting for the reader. He expresses the confusion by fighting the flood of unwanted memories.

And the secret to making something like this work is tied to what I mentioned in the last chapter—allow yourself to become the character as you write. In *Hour of the Scorpion*, it became natural for me to respond the way Jim Tiber does.

A good model for character development in SF is Isaac Asimov's Detective Lije Bailey, from his collection of robot stories, *I, Robot*.

Bailey is very much a human character investigating a murder that occurred in one of the enclosed cities on Earth. But Bailey gets stuck with an android partner who he finds annoying, a disruption in his normal pattern of work.

The conflict between the two of them is what holds our interest as these unlikely partners work together. The android is real to us because we see him through Bailey's annoyed eyes.

In the robot series, Asimov also used his three Laws of Robotics to fuel a wide-variety of intriguing story situations. The laws state that—first—robots cannot harm humans or, through inaction, allow humans to come to harm. The second law says that robots must follow human orders unless those orders come into conflict with the first law. The last law says that a robot must protect its own existence as long as this doesn't conflict with the first or second law.

These simple laws allowed SF Grandmaster Asimov to create a world of intriguing stories. Built into those laws is a cleverly constructed ethical web, one that defines the nature of the inhuman robots. It renders them powerful, but limited in special ways. More importantly, it made the robots *interesting* as characters.

Robert Silverberg's Lord Valentine starts out, in the novel *Lord Valentine's Castle*, as a man with no past and—seemingly—no future. But we sense, from the reactions of other people and of other creatures to Valentine, that he is important.

In fact, Valentine suffers from an induced amnesia, and he has been deprived of his inheritance and his royal birthright. But beyond the story of Valentine's fight to regain his throne, Valentine's amnesiac state serves an important purpose. We get to see the world of Majipoor—all its strange beasts and plants, the many odd races, the whole gigantic planet—through his eyes. Valentine enters the world without his past, so it all seems new to him. He becomes our emissary to that world.

Majipoor would have been too immense a planet to absorb if we, as readers, were just plopped down into it. Through the device of Valentine's amnesia, though, we discover Majipoor along with the protagonist of the book.

A non-human character can be made all the more real if familiar aspects of the creature touch us. Even if they have fur or scales, your characters need to touch the reader. In my novel *The Wizard of Tizare*, Falon, the hero of my book, journeys to an abandoned city and meets a kit, a young cat-like mrem named Ashre, living on his own. The orphan kit leads Falon to his home . . .

> The kit went inside the small house, much like the huts that dotted the hillside of Falon's homeland.
>
> But once inside, Falon saw that it wasn't at all like the cheery homes that he and his friends grew up in. The floor was strewn with a strange assortment of clothes, bits of leathery armor, kilts, scabbards. The wall was filled with weapons, most of them clearly much too heavy for the small mrem to wield. There was a foul, close smell that suggested that the young one didn't know too much about cleaning. Bits of food lay on the floor.
>
> "Your parents?" Falon asked quietly.
>
> Ashre told him, so matter-of-factly, of the last day he saw his mother alive. Quickly, with no feeling. Except— Falon saw him look away, to a small box beside his bed. And Falon could imagine what was there. A lock of her hair, some cherished item that she gave Ashre when he was still suckling on her.

We see Ashre through the eyes of Falon. And we respond to the orphan, his loneliness, and his living by his wits. The image touches us because it *relates* to us. We can respond to what it must be like for a young human, orphaned, perhaps living on the streets. The fact that this is an intelligent animal more like a cat doesn't change that.

No matter *what* the creature is, follow the rules for any well-drawn character. Give them a history.

What did the troll do *before* he started hanging out under the bridge sand-bagging unwary dwarfs? Is that simply the way trolls are, or is this one the product of a bad upbringing? Give the non-human characters flaws. Make the alien proud and boastful, the android insecure. (And know why they're that way.)

Let their personalities follow from their experiences so far. A metamorph's problems may be vastly different than a human's. But think—where would their common ground be? For major non-human characters, write out a full-fledged biography just as you would for a human character, and include the important events in their lives. And always make that history relate to not only who they are, but *what* they are.

For a young dragon, the day he/she gets off their first fiery breath must be an important rite of passage. It could also be the source of some interesting plot twists in case of a mis-fire.

Perhaps nothing is more important than this step of getting the characters right. Beth Fleisher, a former editor at Berkley, says that a science fiction novel must have, "Characters with motivations that make sense . . . as real and credible as possible, no matter how fantastic their world."

Janna Silberstein, editor at Bantam, echoes this. How much the story comes to life "has to do with how much I identify with the characters in the story . . . if I can look at the character and say, wow! That's how I would react."

For author Charles de Lint, the characters are all-important. "I start with the characters," he says. "I have a final scene in mind. I have a mood I want the book to be, I have some thematic concern I want to put across. But other than that, I just start with the characters."

Every SF story will have a different solution to making its characters work. There are no formulas here. But key to the process is being true to the nature of the character, and fixing all the reader's experiences in that point of view.

Exercise

Pick a non-human character from mythology, fairy tale, or legend. Perhaps the troll from *Billy Goats Gruff*, or the wolf in *Red Riding Hood*, maybe the Minotaur guarding the Grecian labyrinth.

Then write a short, one-page scene from that character's point of view. Try to relate to that creature's special perspective. (The troll was hungry. How many days had it been since he heard the sweet sound of a billy goat's hoofs clattering across the bridge? Too many, he thought. . . .)

Keep in mind the character's goals and special problems.

Part 3:

STORYTELLING AND SF

CHAPTER
7

Telling Your Tale

All right. You have a detailed world, and characters who we can identify with and respond to. What else is needed?

But you know the answer to that one. This is the part that you may have thought would come first: creating a story. And here we enter a realm of magic where even the best writing teacher is often silent.

People always ask professional writers . . . say, just where do you get your ideas? In a recent article in *Writer's Digest*, editor/author Thomas Monteleone had some snappy answers.

"There's a mail service I subscribe to," he said . . . "they send ten fresh new ideas each month."

Or there's a little shop in the city that peddles new ideas.

Unfortunately, story ideas come from someplace else—no writers have a clue where. But I do know this: if you walk around, notebook in hand, looking at this world, observing people, places, conflicts—real or imagined—

the story ideas should come. Writers play *what-if* all the time . . .

What if a giant meteor hit Earth? (Pournelle and Niven's *Lucifer's Hammer*.)

What if a super-virus decimated the planet? (Stephen King's *The Stand*.)

What if humankind was suddenly pushed to a new stage of evolution? (Arthur C. Clarke's *Childhood's End*.)

As a SF writer you have to be, well, speculative. You have to look at our mundane, everyday world, the news reports and stories, the articles about scientific research and breakthroughs, the reports on changing social conditions, and then *push* those situations until they become interesting, intriguing, and absorbing.

In the next chapter, I'll document the life cycle of an idea, based on scientific discovery, that became my novel *WURM*. We'll look at it to see what I did to turn fact into fiction, to try and find where the story came from.

But first—let's look at some common story ideas and themes in SF, and see which hoary clichés you should avoid. And why you might not have to . . .

There are stories that immediately trigger groans from editors. For some reason, these ideas seem novel to hopeful writers who haven't done their homework. Take a story like this . . .

Two astronauts become stranded on a new world, their ship destroyed; perhaps their home planet has been completely destroyed. They are alone, and they must start a new life on this world. The male astronaut's name is Adam, and the woman is—

And they called the planet . . . Earth!

I'm sure you get the idea. There are countless variations of that story, and all of them are so familiar that they have passed *way* beyond cliché. They simply aren't acceptable.

Or take this example—please!

A super powerful computer with artificial intelligence is constructed. And said computer proceeds to link up with all electronic aspects of life on earth until—gasp!— it's ready to assume control of the whole planet . . . and the humans become the slaves of the computer.

And perhaps just one more example.

A time traveler goes back in time, and ends up meeting his mother and his father, and has to finagle with events in the past to make sure that he gets born.

Now, if any of these ideas seem particularly novel to you, you simply have not read widely enough in the field. Before you write a word, you should devour short stories and novels in your area, whether it's hard science fiction, science fantasy, pure fantasy, or some hybrid genre. Only by exploring the literature can you know what's been done, and what hasn't been done.

Even though there are story ideas out there so encrusted with barnacles that they simply must be left alone, there are many time-worn themes that welcome a writer attacking them with a new slant.

81

• *Alien worlds* remain a popular jumping-off point for speculative fiction of all kinds. You can explore everything from a Swiftian satire on our own world, to a straight-forward survival epic pitting hapless explorers or colonists against a dangerous inhabitant or environment.

Alien worlds can also be used to create groups of off-world Earthlings whose loyalty may not be to Terra anymore. Dealing with the far future, you can imagine the human race scattered to other planets but still operating with a provincial, and dangerous, mind-set.

• *Over population* used to get more press than it does today, though the figures for the number of people existing at the poverty level, or below, continues to grow. (I read one source indicating that 40 percent of the children in the good old U.S.A. are at the poverty level.)

Conditions in poor areas, such as India and Central Africa, continue to worsen. Where is all this headed, especially when you add the confrontation between the Right to Life groups and the Pro Choice proponents? Is there a Malthusian limit to the resources of the planet, or can we keep an expanding population and eventually meet the needs of all the passengers on spaceship Earth?

Harry Harrison's excellent novel *Make Room, Make Room!* is a classic in the field, but the overpopulation problem he dealt with is much worse today, twenty years later.

• *Powerful computers* would seem to fall into the cliché category. And yes, we probably don't need any more stories of super machines taking over the planet. (But be sure to see my comments at the end of this chapter—just to confuse you completely.)

However, computer chips have completely integrated themselves into our lives, from supermarket checkouts and CD players, to air traffic control and personal fitness evaluations. The computer—to a great extent—has won the battle, and it now "assists" many aspects of our lives.

What is next? One computer scientist I know is working on a computer that you can talk to. In fact, a prototype is up and running, and we're probably only years away from a commercial machine that you will speak to . . . and the keyboard will seem completely antiquated.

Another computer scientist is working on Artificial Intelligence—and he's very secretive about the breakthroughs being made . . . except to tell me that they are getting closer to the goal of having a machine that can really think.

Again, there are no stories here, no plots, no characters. That's your job, to look at the current technology, and then project it in interesting ways, imagining different situations that can engage the reader's interest.

George Alec Effinger's *When Gravity Fails* made use of technological consciousness-altering set against a Middle Eastern background. The computer chip technology isn't central to the story, it's just part of the world.

• *The Apocalypse* has, at times, seemed closer than it does today. Always subject to the winds of political change, our fear of the "End" can vary depending on the world climate.

There are countless visions of the Apocalypse, from a terminal gasoline crisis to an opportunistic disease that claims most of the population of the planet. I grew up with the threat of nuclear war as a very real thing.

Once, as a boy, staying at our beach house, I was awakened by terrible sirens. I shot up in bed, sweating, crying, convinced that the missiles were falling.

Now that fear seems so ancient. Yet the kids of my generation lived with it day to day . . .

Could that kind of threat be made to work again? Possibly, but there are so many more interesting ways to consider an earthly Armageddon. Recently, *The New York Times* Science section ran a feature on the high likelihood (in the next 50 years) of our planet being hit by a major meteor of sufficient size to kill most life on the planet.

And—this is amazing, if hard to believe—you have a *greater* chance of being killed by such a meteor than dying in a plane crash. (But don't worry, that bit of actuarial doom-saying is derived from the statistical fact that one major plane crash kills a few hundred people, while the meteor would take out nearly everyone on the planet.)

Stephen King's *The Stand* was a best-seller both at the time of its original release, in 1978, and then in its unexpurgated, updated version released in 1990. *The Stand* was a remarkably prescient novel, postulating a super virus for which there was no cure. The awareness of the plague of AIDS was still half a decade away.

King's apocalyptic novel mixed the horror of great cities filled with the dead and dying with a fantastic tale of good and evil squaring off for the future of the survivors and the planet.

There are certainly enough threats to our existence today, from ozone layers with gaping holes to toxic dumps leaching into the ground water. As a fictional theme, the Apocalypse remains vital.

• *Quest* tales are perhaps the oldest form of literature. From Odysseus bouncing around in his ship while his wife fights off potential suitors, to the hapless Gawain hunting for the Holy Grail, the quest is a theme that can be done tiredly but can never, itself, be tired.

What do protagonists in SF go questing for . . . ?

Adventure, perhaps, or independence; a lost parent, a lost inheritance, a lost person. The quest can start as a mundane job—travel here and do this—or it can be a noble journey to obtain something, or someone, of vital importance.

Many of the great fantasy novels, such as Tolkien's *Lord of the Rings* trilogy, involve quests for items of great magic, needed to save the race. But many of the

great science fiction masterworks also use the quest as
the centerpiece, the driving force of their plot. Heinlein's *Glory Road* and, in a different way, *Stranger in a
Strange Land*, both involve quests. Asimov's *Foundation*
trilogy uses many quests, from the work of Hari Sel-
don, psychohistorian, to control history, to the Mule,
starting out on an ominous voyage of conquest and
domination.

Quests can be private, internal matters, or they can
be a large-scale activity to save a civilization.

• *Time Travel* remains a popular sub-genre—despite
the fact that the activity of time travel is riddled with
paradoxes and conundrums that make the whole activity totally preposterous.

And though the old time trails have been well-worn,
rendering a lot of story ideas clichés, there are just too
many wonderful things you can do traveling in time
not to include it as a major story theme.

The trick here, of course, is to find something *new* to
do with time travel. My *Time Warrior* series plays with a
group in the future trying to change the outcome of
major battles in the past to shape history to serve their
own purposes. A novel aspect of this series is the fact
that the reader doesn't know whether a specific
event—say, the desert defeat of Rommel, the Tet Of-
fensive, or Pearl Harbor—was supposed to turn out
the way that we know. Real history and the time
travelers' fun and games overlap.

My novel *Darkborn* (Berkley/Diamond) falls, for the

sake of marketing convenience, into the category of horror. And it is the most traditional work that I've done in the field.

But at the same time, the book has a dramatic finish that uses time travel to allow readers first to experience a terrible loss by the protagonist, and then to see that loss removed.

My gut feeling is that the market for time travel stories will always be there—it's just too juicy a topic. But before you start your own generation-spanning epic, start your reading with H.G. Wells' *The Time Machine* (reprinted in 1990 in a new annotated edition from The University of North Carolina Press) and then start working through the literature. For a more modern recommendation, I'd suggest a look at David Gerrold's wonderful *The Man Who Folded Himself*.

• *Alternate Universes/Alternate Realities . . .* The conceit here is that there is another universe, other worlds, beyond the ones that we know. Sometimes the author speculates that these worlds exist side-by-side with ours, accessed by some kind of dimensional door.

In other cases, the alternate universes are simply somewhere *way out there*, in a part of the universe where the normal rules of physics no longer apply.

And while we have had plenty of stories of mirror earths where all the events of our history are slightly "off," the idea of other dimensions and other worlds remains a fun one to explore.

• *New Technology* provides a ready-made source of

inspiration for stories and novels. If you don't subscribe to a scientific journal, such as *Science, The Scientific American, Natural History, Air & Space*, or some other magazine, you're cutting yourself off from a wonderful source of inspiration, and good stories.

The New York Times, for example, features a weekly Science section with articles that keep me inspired with story ideas. There have been features on everything from the mysterious and dangerous wave action in the North Atlantic to a new, easy-as-pie way an H-bomb can be put together.

In 1990, Harvard University Press published a sumptuous book called *The Ants*. The oversized book —with color plates—is nothing less than the definitive study of the communal insect, the ant. Before the book came out, I was researching a computer company's attempts to encourage group problem-solving. With the book on ants, my computer research, and a timely article on gene mapping, I had the makings for a book I hoped to write on the group mind, computer technology, and genetic engineering.

Stay current with fast-moving technology, and the story ideas should leap out at you.

Tell Your Tale

Many writers come to science fiction and fantasy trying to recreate a book or a myth that's been done to death.

Orson Scott Card, author of *Prentice Alvin*, says that, "In far too many novels we end up getting 9th-generation reality."

If you're starting out in the SF market, a fresh story will be very much appreciated . . . not that it can't involve classic touchstones, but you will need an original slant.

There are many ways to go about creating that tale if you don't simply have a fresh vision rumbling around in your mind. First, familiarize yourself with what's on the racks now. Read a few books listed on the LOCUS best-seller list, such as Greg Bear's *Eon*. (See the appendix listing for LOCUS at the end of this book.)

Also, read the established, classic authors such as Asimov, Silverberg, and Heinlein. By looking at what's old and what's new, you'll get some idea of the range and the scope of science fiction and fantasy.

When you have an idea of the type of world you want to write about, perhaps even the characters, play with different possibilities. Brainstorm situations. Take traditional quest stories, and change them around. Let the beautiful princess of the galactic empire rescue the prince. Make a group of aliens loyal supporters of the humans. Have a quest to *return* a powerful object.

Above all, be alert to the conflicts inherent in your world. Silverberg's Majipoor had an entire city devoted to recording its history. And much of the tension rose out of the conflict *inherent* in having six completely different intelligent species on the planet.

If you created, for example, a gravity-free world, think

about the problems that would make your characters' lives very interesting. Perhaps whatever keeps their feet on the ground is being controlled by a religious sect. Or maybe gravity is returning, with some cataclysmic complications. Use the natural tension in your world and in the characters.

But, above all, there *must* be suspense. From the beginning of your story, the reader should feel the tension. A simple enough rule, you might think—but it's the obvious rules that often get broken.

Theme and Scope

It's not enough for you to come up with a neat story idea and some characters to make the action interesting. Oh, you might be able to sell the story or the book, and it might even be fun to read. But—at its heart—if that's *all* you have, the story won't have any meaning beyond the entertainment value of the plot threads that you've woven together.

Your tale needs a theme and scope. By theme, I mean that the story will have to be *about* something . . . something more than conflicts and complications that your protagonist faces.

It could be about the changing nature of our society, as we all retire to our home electronics cocoons, abandoning our less fortunate neighbors. It could be about the importance of sacrificing to save others, or—on the other hand—the need to keep one's own vision, one's goals, uppermost.

It can be about the nature of unconditional love, about the importance of friends, or the pain of loss. You can deal with one big theme, or you can—especially in a novel— deal with a number of smaller themes.

The point is this: you should have something that you want to say in the context of your story. You are not going to be getting on a pulpit, but the tale should have a subtext if you want it to reverberate and touch readers in anything more than a visceral way.

One way to do this is to add something to the biography of your major characters, kind of an "internal goals" statement. What will the character learn, or try to accomplish, in the course of the story? Will they learn the value of loving someone? Can you use a character's xenophobia to make a statement about intolerance? Perhaps your characters will learn the importance of protecting our world.

And don't neglect the antagonists in your story. Their inner goals might be less pleasant—like removing any competing species from the universe—but that *idée fixe* is still part of the story.

Your story should also have *scope*. We should get a sense that there are issues, ideas, subplot threads, and aspects of characters and the worlds that, while they aren't central to the story, are still present.

If you set a story on contemporary Earth, for example, you should include material that roots it to our time, with the social issues and concerns of that time. The same applies to a story set in the future or on another world. While you want to tell the story from a few important points of view, you need the reader to feel that world and its time.

Is there injustice, social unrest, emotional and political issues? Let them filter through the story, adding depth to your book, broadening its scope.

All of this can be serious business. In her book *The Devil's Arithmetic*, Jane Yolen uses time travel to let readers experience the Holocaust through a contemporary young girl's eyes. Yolen used the SF novel to make a terrible and important time come to life for young readers.

"Fantasy and science fiction," Yolen has said, "can deepen our response to realism."

And though I have cautioned you about time-worn stories and themes, keep in mind that, with the right approach, yesterday's clichés can be made fresh. James Cameron's film *Terminator 2* uses a number of time travel and computer clichés—including a whopper of a paradox that makes the first film completely impossible.

But, in combination, the ideas take on a fresh look, and the film excited audiences who came back for repeat viewings.

Jane Yolen told me that, "Anything can be done again if done well." Editor Beth Fleisher said, "I don't see any idea that is ready for the mothballs."

"You never know. . . ," Charles de Lint said. "Someone

might come along with something so fresh and new with dwarves and castles and unicorns. Look at Michael Bishop's *Unicorn Mountain*."

The trick is, of course, to make the story your own. Do your research, build your world, really develop characters we can relate to.

And then weave a multi-level plot with as much suspense as you can.

Exercise

Quickly sketch out a one-page outline of a story, perhaps using the world and characters you've already created. Be alert to opportunities for your story to say something beyond the mere turns of the plot.

CHAPTER
8

The Life Cycle of WURM—
From an Idea to a Book

I travel with a note pad.

Actually, it's a small spiral note pad inside a leatherette folder. My wife gave me a pair of those folders for Christmas, and there are pockets to slip in pieces of paper torn from the tiny pad, and another place for ticket stubs, business cards, and other bits of loose paper.

These note pads are absolutely vital to my business. I may not know where the story ideas come from, but I sure know what to do once I get them.

There was a time when I'd go on a hike and not have a way to jot down an idea. Once, I got an idea for a story while climbing Anthony's Nose, a small mountain in the Hudson Highlands.

I was afraid that if I didn't record this idea it would vanish forever.

So I picked up two stones—one was a flatish piece of slate. And then I proceeded to carve a little memo to myself in the rock.

It was a primitive moment, to be sure. But it was also

wonderful—since it showed the exhilarating power of an idea, the tantalizing vision it gives of a story that could be.

Now I travel with my note pads—everywhere. And most ideas get scribbled down and don't seem particularly impressive afterwards. Often, I'll stare at my notes for a story idea, scratch my head, and wonder just what I had been so excited about.

But other times, something more magical happens.

And that's what this chapter is about . . .

Where WURM Came From

A few years back there was a PBS special on *wunderkind* Robert Ballard's exploration of the hydrothermal vents in the Mid-Atlantic and the Gulf of Mexico. Ballard is the glamorous oceanographer-cum-submersible jockey who brought back live footage of the Titanic; we got to see the legendary ship lying on the bottom, an algae-encrusted hulk.

So much for romance.

On his more recent trip, Ballard went to the open volcanic seeps that run along the deep ocean fault lines, and he brought back incredible footage, shots that were like scenes from another planet.

Surrounding the incredibly hot vents, scientists found a completely novel life system, as alien as anything they'd ever dreamed of finding on another world.

There were giant albino crabs, monster-sized clams,

weird, oversized mussels, sea cucumbers, and giant brittle sea stars. But the most amazing animals were the giant tube worms, worms with a reddish tinge, that could grow to twenty feet or more. These giant tube worms had a parasitic core, a colony-creature within a creature, and scientists didn't know which was host and which was resident. The most bizarre thing about the giant tube worms was their reddish color—and the reason why they have that color. The parasites at the core of the tube worms are chemosynthesizers. They don't partake in the Earth's sunny photosynthetic existence. The parasitic core of the tube worms takes the poisonous sulfur dioxide produced by the vents and, with the intense heat bubbling from the volcanic fissures, they produce food.

With no light.

They are an alien life form. And there is also this odd fact—the tube worms have that reddish tinge because their bodies have a substance that closely matches hemoglobin.

Perhaps you begin to get the picture.

As striking as such a vision is, it still wasn't a book idea. But it was something that I filed away inside my mind.

The book idea came to me years later. I was sitting in a beach chair at our New Jersey beach house, watching my two kids, making sure that they didn't drown. I listened to the repetitive crash of the waves, I watched the sun glare off the water, the hundreds of people at the shore . . . and I thought about *all* the beaches in the world.

And I thought about the giant tube worms of the hydrothermal vents. They were an alien life form, confined to an alien environment of heat and chemicals.

I wondered what a real opportunistic chemosynthesizer might do—how it would be able to go directly to a living source for its chemical nutrients, for its hemoglobin. What if the tube worms could live on the surface—if they could carry out their parasitic activities with other living things?

I watched my children running in and out of the surf, laughing, giggling. The dominant life forms on our planet are made up of photosynthesizers, and those that feed off the food produced by the photosynthesizers.

Was there a point in evolution, though, at which the development could have gone the other way? Could that primeval battle be joined again?

Then there were two other new wrinkles. A dozen years ago, the Coney Island Aquarium, a wonderful place located in the faded wonderland that is Coney Island today, displayed a truly bizarre creature.

An expedition to the Gulf of Mexico had discovered a two-foot-long albino aquatic isopod, a giant pill bug. The strange animal looked as though it should have been long extinct. And though the creature was alive when I saw it, all the specimens later died within months of being brought back to the pressurized tanks.

Autopsies revealed a strange diet—a mixture of shellfish (with their shells!), sea stars, and other creatures from the abyssal depths.

And this provided the key to the plot of *WURM*, the

reason the worms have been limited to their severe environment.

I speculated that if there were two antagonistic life systems on the planet—maybe this battle was very old. Maybe it had happened before, on a large scale.

That, in sketch form, was the story idea behind my book. And now the real work had to be done.

Researching *WURM*

Since *WURM* was going to be rooted in a new scientific discovery, I wanted to get the facts right, since the very strangeness of that reality would add to my book.

I got hold of a copy of the original PBS special on Ballard, which revived my memory of those tube worms. Ballard's expedition had been sponsored by the Woods Hole Oceanographic Institution.

I called up Woods Hole and spoke with the person who handled their public relations. Most large institutions have someone whose job is to talk to the press.

I explained what my project entailed, and the helpful PR person sent along a packet including a background booklet on the Institution, detailed sketches and color slides of the submersible, *Alvin*, and the robot sleds used to film in deep ocean.

My office walls became filled with photographs of the subs, the camera sleds, and the research vessel they operated from.

But the most important thing they sent me was a copy of the magazine, *Oceanus*, devoted to the study of the ocean. This issue focused on the deep-sea hot springs, and featured photos of the expedition studying the vent creatures. There were charts showing the relative sizes of the animals, and the chemical composition of the water near the seeps.

Wonderful photos showed rift worms after they were brought to the surface, their bodies destroyed by the change in pressure. And—since this was all new to the scientists—there were articles explaining how these strange creatures fit into the evolutionary history of earth.

All of this was very exciting.

But I knew that a place modelled on Woods Hole would figure into my book. While seeing pictures of the submersibles was good, I felt that I should go there in person.

I took a trip to Woods Hole, drove down to the docks, saw the research vessel and the submersibles—all images that would be vital to the writing of my book.

My next goal was to try to track down more information about the giant isopod that the Coney Island Aquarium had displayed years ago. Again, I called the Aquarium and got someone whose job was to speak to the media. I asked about the strange creature—and for a few minutes, I drew a blank.

The media person was new, and didn't recall any such creature. But then he asked the director, and came back to the phone, telling me that he had a file filled with photographs and information.

He shipped that information off to me, and the albino isopod glared out at me, grimly, while I worked.

Now, while all this research was going on, the story idea of *WURM* was being altered, modified by the research. Full-blown scenes suggested themselves . . . a test carried out in the Coney Island Aquarium, and a dive in the submersibles to the deep-sea hot springs, the research vessel steaming into Falmouth Harbor—with no one left on board.

In other words, the research began to shape the sketchy story ideas, adding complications and deepening the concept.

One of the most thrilling parts of this research was when I tried to obtain a copy of the map of the ocean floor. A good part of the action of the book would take place in the deep sea, and I wanted to see the ocean floor, to have a map of it, just as I would of any other location that I was writing about.

Through various sources, I learned that the famous map of the ocean floor was available from a woman in Nyack, New York, named Marie Tharp. The reason she was able to sell the map was that she, along with the late Bruce Heezen, had created the map from information supplied by the U.S. Navy and other sources.

Not only that, Tharp discovered the Mid-Atlantic Ridge, the massive underwater mountain chain that separated the Old World from the New.

When I called up to order my map, I got to speak with Tharp about her discovery. Here was someone who uncovered one of the great geological features of the planet by plotting data on a map.

That interview inspired a number of scenes featuring scientists working both above and below the surface, studying the Wurm . . .

The World of WURM

The research of WURM led to the creation of the world of WURM.

Coney Island became a major setting—the Aquarium, the grungy amusement area, the carousel that's open year-round, the smell of fudge and salt water.

A place very much like Woods Hole was used, as well as a research vessel. Other settings included Manhattan, Flamingo Harbor in Florida, and Rome. In all these cases, the locations were places that I had visited, and that I knew.

But there was one place that I couldn't visit, that I could only know through film and videotape. That was the deep sea, the black, nightmarish environment where monstrous fishes dangle phosphorescent lures to angle for smaller prey. A field trip with Robert Ballard was out of the question.

But still there were things I could do to make that world come to life. I watched documentaries on the deep ocean. I read Ballard's account of his discovery of the Titanic. *Oceanus* magazine had a number of detailed accounts of dives in the submersible *Alvin*.

The rest would depend on my imagination . . .

The Characters of *WURM*

Though I had the outline of a story and locations, the plot of the book was still sketchy.

And that's as it should be. Now was the time to create the characters who would be the eyes for the reader, the point of view characters, who would experience the story of *WURM*.

Some of the decisions seemed pre-ordained. There was Dr. Michael Cross, director of the New York Aquarium. There was a bull-headed scientist based at the Oceanographic Institution, at odds with Cross. Their conflict would be over the danger posed by this new form of life.

Then there were character decisions that may have seemed arbitrary, but reflected my desire to make this a human story as well as a technical one.

Cross is divorced, and his daughter, Jo, lives with his ex-wife, Caryn, in Manhattan. Jo is a stubborn girl, used to getting her own way. That stubbornness, her natural curiosity, draws the reader's concern. She spends two weeks each summer with her father . . . and this is the summer her father uncovers the secret of the Wurm.

There were a few other key characters, such as Michael Cross's research assistant, who experiments on himself to determine how to stop the spread of the chemo-synthesizers, and Jo's friends, who try to keep her from her rash impulsive acts.

But I limited the points of view to three or four key point of view characters. Their relationships to each other carry built-in tensions and complications that suggested sub plots that would, with luck, make the tension of *WURM* very high.

Writing the Book

Now—with the world and the characters, I was ready for the story. I started by jotting down every possible event that I could envision happening in the book.

I didn't do this in any particular order. I just jotted down ideas on a yellow pad that was quickly filled with plot points, some major, some minor, some adding defini-tion to the characters, others introducing information.

Some of these events were mutually exclusive, and decisions would have to be made about the direction I'd take the book.

Still other possible scenes would be accepted and then abandoned during the actual writing of the book.

When I had exhausted plot ideas, scenes, and whatever small events I had noted, I wrote each event on a small strip cut from an index card. I labeled the event as to whether it fit in the beginning, middle, or end of the book. I also noted whether it was from an early section or late section of the book.

An event, for example, could be coded B3, meaning towards the end of the beginning of the book.

When I had all the cards in order, with some events still mutually exclusive, I took the cards, now in order, and copied them onto a series of file folders, outlining the novel from the beginning and the end.

I left plenty of room for writing notes, questions, and reminders to myself. Some plot developments just wouldn't develop. Other, newer scenes would take the place of planned events.

And finally I was ready to write.

Writing and Selling *WURM*

These two subjects each deserve their own chapter, but—to finish the story of the *WURM* novel, let me add a few remarks.

As is always the case with my work, I had my agent sell the book before I started writing it. Some authors prefer writing the complete novel, and then marketing it. But I'm far too insecure for that.

The agent returned with a two-book contract from the publisher, and I was off and running.

The actual writing of the novel took over three months, with another few weeks for revisions. Keep in mind that I write full-time, and I tend to write quickly. Many writers will take up to a year on a novel.

The book was well received by the editor. But she did

ask for a cut of 10,000 words, since it would otherwise have been well over 400 pages long.

The first cuts I made took away important scenes—a fact that was discovered when I let my wife read the revised version of the book. With a bit more tinkering I removed the words without damaging the story.

WURM went on to garner the best reviews of my career thus far, and was a best seller on *Mystery Scene* magazine's list.

But—by then—I was already at work developing and writing a new novel . . . and *WURM* seemed like a dream from long ago.

Exercise

Pick a topic from a science magazine or article, and then learn more about it. Contact first-hand sources, and call the museum or the school involved. Get background information beyond what appeared in the article.

And—to be sure—jot down any story ideas you get.

CHAPTER
9

On Writing and SF

There is one loud and clear complaint I hear from editors about new science fiction and fantasy novels.

There's a couple of things that are vital to your SF tale, whether it's a novel or a story. You need a multi-level plot, fresh and exciting, with involving characters. But above all there must be *suspense*. Almost from the beginning, the reader should feel the tension—a simple enough rule, you might think.

Jane Yolen, the writer who edits her own line of books for Harper-Collins, says that "half the novels have no tension in them at all." It's not enough to have the language, the characters, and the setting appropriate to your theme. You need to hook the reader.

Here's a scene from my novel, *Cloud Captain*. The setting is Mars, at the end of the 19th century. The British sail full-rigged cloudships across the hostile planet carved from the imagination of H. G. Wells and Jules Verne. The captain is on a rope ladder, inspecting the vital lift panels that make the ship "fly" . . .

Colin returned his attention to the port lift panels.

"They look just fine—" he started to say.

He felt the smallest shift of the rope ladder. Just a fraction of an inch, but enough to make him clutch the ladder harder while his breath caught in his throat.

He looked up.

And near the top of the ladder, he saw the cause. One rung down from the deck, the rope ladder was almost completely frayed away.

No, he thought. *Not* frayed. This heavy Martian hemp, made from the incredibly tough and reedy plant that grows along the cabal swamps, wouldn't just fray.

It had been cut.

Just enough so he could get on the rope and snap it . . .

As one editor said to me, tension is the craft of writing—but that may be easier said than done. What is the magic element that makes us flip the pages of one book and then barely drag ourselves through another?

Here are some guidelines to creating suspense and tension in your SF.

• *Make the reader care immediately.*

People don't pick up science fiction and fantasy for a casual read, dozing off in their easy chair while Phil Donahue drones on in the background.

SF readers want to be involved in your world and the lives of your characters. You have the hard task of making the reader concerned about things which don't exist. I have already spoken about the importance of making that world as real, and the characters as empathetic, as possible. If you've done your work there, you should be ready, from the start of the book, to grab the reader's attention and hold it.

In the beginning of my novel *WURM*, something happens to the robotically operated vehicle (ROV) a mile under the sea. The ROV, dubbed "Lil Shit," hits an undersea cliff filled with giant tube worms, and then all the video cameras go dead. The crew of the research ship topside has to drag the ROV up . . .

It was raining, a warm, almost soothing tropical rain.

But it made it difficult for Simonsen to see anything, the sheets of water running off his glasses.

I need goddamn windshield wipers, he thought.

Jane North stood next to him. She was feeling bad, he guessed. It wasn't her fault, but if the ROV didn't pop to the surface, she'd end up blaming herself.

"Where do you guess she'll surface?" he asked.

Normally she could sit at the console and guide Lil Shit right next to the ship.

"I don't know. Not too far away from the ship. She was about at the end of her tether."

He nodded. The captain was on the deck ready to get the submersible on board just as soon as it surfaced.

They waited. And Simonsen had just about lost hope.

When the bright red dome of the ROV broke the rough surface.

Everyone clapped and whistled. The captain wasted no time getting the Achilles alongside. And Simonsen looked over at the ROV, just the upper few inches of its dome-like body bobbling on top of the water. The surface was all scratched, like it had been scraped with a knife, or a razor, over and over, a maze-like pattern.

The captain lowered the hook of the winch.

The hook slid past the lifting bail. Once, then again. But then the ROV was finally hooked and Simonsen gave Tom the signal to haul away.

The churning sea splashed against the ship, against Lil Shit. Everyone was soaked.

But everyone wanted to see what had happened to the submersible. It popped out of the water. Streams of water rolled away from it.

"Holy shit," Reilly said.

The arm was still extended. Still extended, but twisted at a sick angle. It was broken, damn it.

But that's not what Reilly was excited about.

There was a chunk of the worm still held tightly to the manipulator arms.

"We've got a piece of it!" he yelled over the wind and the rain. He hurried to a sullen Jane North and gave her a hug. "Way to go doll, even if you did fuck up Lil Shit."

The ROV dangled in the air, still over the water, and after a moment's pause, the captain swung it over onto the main deck, beside Prom II.

Simonsen kept looking at the chunk of worm.

Well, that's good, he thought, glad to have a piece of it.

But there was something about it that bothered him.

He watched Lil Shit come to a gentle landing on a wooden pallet.

Reilly hurried to the front of the ROV.

There was something wrong . . .

Reilly knelt down, next to the broken manipulator, a big grin plastered on his soaking face.

Simonsen took a step close to him.

And he remembered.

He had seen Riftia worms brought to the surface before. And he remembered how they looked all squashed, exploded by the change in pressure. Every cell of their bodies dead.

But this worm looked different.

It looked—Alive . . .

The smell, the rotten egg smell, was strong, even while the wind blew the warm rain into their faces. It was the stench of sulfur. Powerful but familiar . . . expected.

But this was too strong. He could taste it!

"Ed, don't you think you better get some gloves, a specimen bag, some—"

And he thought . . . Everything dies when it's brought to the surface. Everything.

Simonsen took another step. "Ed . . ."

But this piece of the worm wasn't dead. No, he could see that. The way it shimmered, rippling, moving in the pincer grip of the manipulator's claw.

"Don't," he started to say. "Don't touch that."

But Reilly's hand had already grabbed the worm, its thick body. He was grinning at his prize . . . not seeing it move, not caring—

"Don't!" Ed yelled again.

But it was, of course, too late . . .

If I did my job, if the characters and the sea setting were real, the readers will want to know what happens next.

• *Tighten the tension*

The readers want to know what happens next—but that doesn't mean that you have to tell them. Assuming that you have created a spark of interest—Say, what's going to happen to those guys on the ship? Gee, how bad is it that they brought the worm on board the ship?

Now is not the time to tell them.

In the very next chapter of *WURM*, I cut away from that action, moving to Coney Island and the Aquarium Director on a jog around Coney. It's a big jump, and it risks being seen as disconcerting. Especially since I don't get back to the ship at sea until chapters later . . . and by then, well—

That big leap—geographically and thematically—signals that the scope of my story is big . . . that whatever will happen on the Research Vessel is important.

But that wouldn't be enough. Having one suspenseful ball in the air isn't *nearly* enough. Now, with my other main characters, I introduce two or three different lines of tension. The Aquarium Director's daughter decides that this is the day she's going to feed the sharks, although she's been warned not to. And there is conflict between the Aquarium Director and his board.

And with each thread of plot laid down, I raise issues that we want to see resolved—and don't. At least not for a long time, and by then I've introduced new, more important concerns.

First worrying about the crew exposed to a strange life form, then about a strong-willed girl who gets in trouble, *WURM* eventually has the fate of the world as its concern. But such concern, and the tension that goes with it, is built a layer at a time.

• *Leave Unfinished Business*

. . . at the end of chapters, that is. The same approach could be applied to short stories . . . if you break your story into sections and have each section end with unfinished business, a cliff-hanger.

In my story "The Murderer," for Robert Silverberg's *Time Gate II* anthology, I made sure that each section of this story of a high-tech hunt for Jack the Ripper ended with a hook, leading the reader to the next section. Here, a wealthy man, Porter, is about to try out his computer reconstruction of London at the time of the Ripper . . .

Vinson reached over and grabbed the two gloves that were perfectly fitted for Porter's meaty hands. He helped Porter slip them on. They were, of course, custom made, extra large, incredibly responsive to even the smallest movements.

Porter would be able to control his recreated world with incredible ease.

It's sick, Vinson thought. This whole thing . . . Porter, his incredible money, this project . . . the years of work simply to—

The screen cleared. There was nothing there.

"Vinson . . ." Porter croaked, unable to contain his excitement. "Where is it? Show it to me! Show me London!"

Vinson laughed. "It's in your hands, Mr. Porter. Just clench your fists . . . just once."

And Vinson grinned as he watched Porter make a fist, and the holotank filled with the murky fog of London . . .

The section of the story ends there. There's a break in the text, and then the new section starts. That break, the pause, makes us hold our breaths along with Porter.

There are, by the way, a few other things to note about the above section. First, it is written from Vinson's point of view. It is the wealthy Mr. Porter who hopes to spot Jack the Ripper, but we see him and his excitement through the eyes of the technician, Vinson. To a large extent, Vinson reflects our attitudes toward the project, and he shapes our feelings.

And you'll also note truncated sentences and ideas. We tend to speak and think in fragments, leaving a lot unsaid and un-thought. Using that technique in your writing draws the reader into the work. Everything isn't spelled out; the reader has to do some thinking, and sometimes it doesn't hurt to have them confused as to just what it is that's not being said.

It's a common device, but one well worth learning how to master.

113

• *Place Important Characters at Risk*

There is nothing wrong with having a minor character in danger. Often, to emphasize the stakes in a situation, you need bad things to happen to minor characters.

But it's your main characters, your point of view characters, whom we have to care about. They are the ones that must have something to gain or lose. In *Lucifer's Hammer*, Niven and Pournelle have a large cast of characters dealing with the impending disaster of the meteor. But only a few of those characters are important to us, and those we know well.

And it bears repeating that in a novel, and certainly in a short story or a novella, you must limit your point of view characters to three or four. Remain faithful to each point of view. Let readers experience everything through that character's eyes, memories, and feelings.

• *Make the atmosphere strong*

You can have a fully developed world but still, in individual paragraphs or sections, have the overall feeling fall flat. It will be hard to hook readers into your story if the background, the atmosphere, is stale. And all the detail that you created in Chapter Three won't help you here.

You need to be involved in the scenes with all your senses. The opening scenes of a chapter or a section should be immediately vivid. Creating a definite sense of mood, expectation, and place is always important in good SF writing, but take special care with your opening. Use all of your point of view characters' senses to make the reader picture *everything* as clearly as possible. Later in your book, a breakneck plot may not allow, or need, such detail. But in the beginning it's absolutely crucial.

• *Let Your Characters Do the Doubting*

When you're dealing with speculative fiction, with speculative ideas, technology, and themes, there will be natural resistance on the part of the reader. They have to be convinced of the reality of your story.

In Michael Crichton's *Jurassic Park* (1990), dinosaurs are cloned and a theme park is set up in an island in South America. The idea initially sounds preposterous, but Crichton's background work on gene mapping and the presence of DNA in fossilized material is convincing. It's made all the more convincing by a cast of characters who doubt the whole procedure, and who question with growing incredulity every aspect of the project. So, even as Crichton gives us hard information documenting the project, key characters first doubt it and then become convinced—usually, long after the reader.

Using characters to do the doubting takes away that option from the reader. Done well, with realistic background and well-researched information, such characters can make the reader join with the writer in creating a speculative world.

115

Peter Benchley's 1991 best-seller, *Beast*, speculates about a creature that has rarely been seen: the Giant Squid. Little is known about the creature, but Benchley is able to mix what facts are known with his own fictional creations to create a powerful menace from the sea. While most characters doubt the presence of such a creature, we have long since been convinced by Benchley.

In my novel *Sleep Tight* (and please skip the next paragraph if you plan on picking up the book—I'd hate to spoil any of your fun), the characters, and thereby the readers, are told by a scientist that some terribly twisted creatures from distant galaxies have opened a passageway into the small town of Harley-on-Hudson. The doddering professor patiently explains that the creatures have tried to enter before . . . destroying the Aztecs, devouring the Roanoke Colony, and crashing into the Tuguska Forest in Siberia. Everyone ridicules the scientist, laughing at his preposterous ideas—while all the while we know, yes, clever us, we *know* that the old boy is right on the money. Their disbelief in the face of so much evidence makes us accept the whole premise.

Letting your characters disbelieve . . . question . . . doubt every incredible thing that happens, puts readers on the side of the story—just where you want them.

• *Writing—101*
Suspense and suspension of disbelief are important.

But, needless to say, you better have the basics down. Grammar, sentence structure, spelling, and format are all important. Strunk & White's oft-recommended title, *The Elements of Style*, is a must-have for any writer. A book like *The New York Times Manual of Style and Usage* can also be helpful.

Write with a good dictionary and thesaurus in hand. Many word processing programs feature spelling dictionaries and a thesaurus. A few programs even offer a style checker which will give you a report on wordiness, word repetition, and clumsy sentence structure.

Do what you can, either through studying style books or using computer aids, to make sure that your writing is as seamless as possible, and that it's your ideas, story, characters, and themes that will be scrutinized—and not your gaffes.

Don't be afraid to ape another writer's style. Imitation is not only the sincerest form of flattery—it's also a good way to discover the stylistic tricks developed by another writer. You will have to find your own voice, but that should come through a lot of experimentation.

Remember my comments about truncated sentences and speeches cut off in mid-sentence. The same applies to your writing. Beginning writers tend to overwrite. Instead, consider that less is more. You can always go back to your text, and add details and facts that might be crucial.

And when you've taken care of all of the above, then you'll be ready for the greatest challenge of all . . .

Part 4:

THE
BUSINESS OF
WRITING

CHAPTER
10

Selling Science Fiction and Fantasy

Writing and selling your stories and novels are two completely different things.

You can simply write your tales, share them with writer's groups and friends, and enjoy the satisfaction of being a creator. But once you decide that another component is needed, that you want, *need*, a larger audience for your work, you enter a completely different realm.

Unless you're very lucky, selling your work will be painful. You'll need perseverance, and an ability not only to shrug off rejection, but to embrace every rejection letter as another benchmark of your career.

You'll get letters that state, "Dear writer, thank you for your recent submission. Unfortunately, it doesn't meet our editorial requirements at this time."

And then you may get a personal note scrawled on a form letter—a bit of a real response, some bona fide feedback, information you can use to make your next effort better.

Then you may even get a real letter back, with words of

advice or encouragement. "This story isn't right, but do try us again."

And you're close now, so close that the rejections have turned into prizes. And then, if you still persevere and if you have some talent, the day will come when someone— they will seem god-like to you—actually buys your story or your novel.

And it will seem that the gates of Paradise have flown open.

Which is about as far from the truth as it can be. But that struggle—the realities of being a professional SF writer—deserves a book of its own. For now, let's look at what you can do to make that day arrive.

• *Start Writing (and Keep Writing)*

To be a writer means that you have to be disciplined. You can't wait for the muse to bestow wonderful ideas on you, firing you with an irresistible desire to write.

You have to plant your butt in a chair, and pound out words. If you plan on cracking the short story market, write stories, revise them, put them aside, and then start other stories. Go back to old stories. When you think you have a story good enough, send it out. (For places to send it, see below.)

If you plan on writing novels, set a word count for every day. Five hundred words, 1000, 1500 . . . Set a figure, and see whether it seems reasonable. And then, make sure you stick to your schedule. There's no point in getting involved in this if you can't make yourself work in a hard and consistent way.

Many writers want to jump in and write novels right away.

It's what I did.

And it didn't work. Over a dozen years ago I produced a first novel that got some good rejection letters and a near-sale. Looking at it now, I can see that it was very rough, unpolished. Worse, I didn't have my own voice, my own style of writing. The novel was written in a generic style following a formula.

But then I started writing articles for magazines. These pieces weren't even fiction, but they let me experiment with storytelling, relating anecdotes, exaggerating them. Somewhere in the process, I started getting big sales to places like *Sports Illustrated, The Los Angeles Times,* and—ultimately—a four-year stint of regular columns in *Isaac Asimov's SF Magazine* and *Analog Science Fiction/Science Fact.*

And then I was ready to try the novel again, and this time it sold quickly, an overnight success that came after years of work.

• *Study the Markets*

There are probably countless beginning writers who write a SF story and immediately fire it off to Ellen Datlow, fiction editor at *Omni.*

Except *Omni* publishes just a few pieces of fiction

each month, and they pay absolute top dollar. They get the best, the biggest names in science fiction and fantasy. And though I'm sure that Ellen Datlow or her assistant still glance at what's called the "slush pile"— the stack of unsolicited manuscripts—the possibility of your gem, if it is a gem, emerging is close to nil.

The big science fiction and fantasy markets pay well. These are magazines found on newsstands throughout the country. But they are also going to be the toughest to break into.

Focus instead on smaller magazines, some that pay only in copies. Use these magazines to make your first sales, getting a track record. From those tiny magazines, you can graduate to what are called semi-pro magazines that may actually pay a half cent or so a word. Gather more credits, so that when you do send a story to one of the big magazines—or when you do send your novel proposal in—you can list a body of work that people have bought and published.

In the appendix, I list some magazines, big and small, and resources to find other magazines.

• *Licensed Worlds*

Many writers want to contribute to Star Trek, Star Wars, or some other mythos. In general, it will be very hard, if not impossible, to do this. The authors of these books are usually hired specifically for these books, and the publishers, working in tandem with Hollywood, want established authors who work fast and well.

Still, it is possible. Pocket Books, who publish the Star Trek books, will gladly send you submission guidelines. These guidelines clearly state that any proposal for Star Trek books must come from an author's agent.

The guidelines tell you what hackneyed plots to avoid—such as travelling in time to change history. The guidelines also lay down strict rules for handling the characters—no relatives or family members not already mentioned in the TV show or films, and no unusual sexual relationships.

It would be a hard market for a beginning writer, but if it's your goal, you will need to get an agent first.

• *About the Novel . . .*

Do you have to write the complete novel before you sell it?

In general, I'd say no. If you have followed the suggestion to sell short fiction to the small markets, then some of the larger ones, you can sell a novel with what's called a "proposal."

Write three chapters of your SF novel. The first three, not the *best* three. An editor wants to be drawn into the book from the beginning. Then write a synopsis of the rest of the book. (But first see my advice below.)

Then query editors with what's called, yes, a query letter. In the query letter, you open with a few exciting sentences taken from your book. Then, in the next paragraph, you give a brief three-sentence summary of the book. The last paragraph is where you list your qualifications for writing this book which should include (a) any personal expertise you have that has a bearing on the book (for example, if you are a scuba diver and your book takes place underwater) and (b) your publishing experience. (And here is where you list your best sales, even offering to send tear sheets of the magazines.)

Just send the letter. I've heard other authors and editors advise simply sending the proposal, and that might also work. But I like sending the query letter, with a SASE, and getting the editor to say a simple, "yes, send the proposal." I then start out with a certain level of interest by holding back the actual proposal.

If the editor is interested, they will ask for the proposal. And if they like that—and you haven't a great deal of experience—the editor will ask for a completed book. There are no guarantees here, but now you will write the book with the active participation of an editor. Often they will make suggestions so that the finished work better suits their editorial needs. You'll be writing knowing that they're interested, and perhaps you'll have a better idea of just what kind of book they want.

And who knows? Your proposal might be strong and compelling enough to convince an editor to make an offer for the novel even before you finish it.

When writing sample chapters for your first novel,

preview the *feel* of the whole book. Let the editor meet the main characters, and get a real sense of who they are. Get your main story line going, as well as any important secondary plot lines.

Then, in the synopsis, tell the editor the rest of the plot, and explain the interpersonal relationship of the characters. Melissa Ann Singer, an editor at Tor Books, suggests devoting about two paragraphs to each chapter.

And no editor wants numbered outlines that resemble your high school social studies report on Ecuador. So, the style of writing should be straightforward. Writing synopses isn't easy. But a good synopsis can help when you write the book, giving you a road map.

"Basically," says Berkley editor Ginjer Buchanan, "the synopsis tells you where the story is going to go . . . though not all authors really know where it's going to end up."

And don't tease the editor. Unlike prospective readers skimming back-cover blurbs, editors must know the whole *story*. Not just the beginning, or the middle, but the very end. And if you don't know how your book will end, don't bother sending in the proposal.

Such coy proposals die a quick death. Tor's Melissa Singer says that she dislikes it when "The author plays games with me and doesn't tell me enough about the story. The ending is the most important part of the book."

• *Get the Format Right*

It would seem a simple enough matter to get the format down, to show how your story or book proposal should look. The *Writer's Market* (see the appendix) has a whole section on proper formats for submissions, but I'll review the basic points here.

Everything should be typed. (But you knew that, didn't you?) Your query letter should have three to four paragraphs of a few sentences each. I prefer not to indent the paragraphs and, instead, separate them by a space.

The book proposal cover page for your story should look like this:

Matthew J. Costello
22 Piping Rock Drive
Ossining, NY 10562   © 1991 M.J. Costello
(phone #)   2976 words

STRANGER THAN FICTION

a story
by

Matthew J. Costello

Note that the margins are about an inch and a quarter on the left, and an inch on the right. After the author's name, address, and copyright information, skip about one-third of the page before listing the title and the type of material (short story, book proposal, etc.).

The story or proposal can begin just below the title, but I usually prefer to begin on the next page.

Of course the manuscript should be clean, with no spelling errors or typos. Use a computer to spell-check your work and catch typos. Include a SASE.

And don't sit around waiting. There are many markets out there—start thinking about them.

• *Make Contact*

Science Fiction and Fantasy is a world that lives on conventions. A SF con, as it is called, is part circus, part huckster fest, and usually entertaining. There are panels with famous and would-be famous authors covering topics as varied as "Women in SF" to "Alternate Histories" and "Humor in Fantasy."

The dealer's room is the place to buy current and out-of-print books, and it's also where attendees generally mingle.

There are often art shows and movies and role-playing games and masquerades, all themed to the many worlds of science fiction and fantasy.

But most important, cons are places where you can meet other writers and editors. Often, there are open parties and book signings. You can press the flesh, smile, and get to meet an editor to whom you might want to sell a book project or a story.

While the convention isn't a place to do business, it

is a place to meet someone that you can write later. You can learn what an editor's likes and dislikes are (and believe me, most editors have very clear ideas of what they do and don't appreciate in writing).

If you do meet an editor and chat for a few minutes, it's something you can mention in a follow-up letter. ("I enjoyed meeting you at Wizardcon. And I thought I'd send along my new novel proposal, *Cyberplanet*.")

You can also meet writers at a con and talk with them. While they are often too busy to look at work—and it's an unfair thing to ask—you can certainly contact them and ask for a friendly recommendation in terms of a good publishing house for SF, or an agent. Sometimes an author will offer to do more. We all remember what it's like to try and break in.

Charles de Lint says, "Don't bring your manuscript. Don't bother people. Just try and get to meet the editors . . . and the various people in the business. It's going to come up in conversation that you've started, or you have completed, a novel or a story. The personal contact is important."

Lastly, the convention will give you a feel for the massive world of SF, the different branches, and the people who write and edit SF.

• *Don't Worry About an Agent*

A few years ago, I met a woman who had completed a SF novel and was frantically trying to interest an agent in handling it.

130

I shook my head, and patiently tried to explain to her that no really good agent would be interested in an unpublished author—and any agent who was probably wouldn't be able to do anything for her.

Still, she had been sending out her manuscript and cover letters to one agent after the other.

I told her she should put that effort into selling her book. Then—after a publisher nibbles—she'd have no problem getting an agent.

It was hard convincing her, but eventually my message got through. The woman started sending out her sample chapters to publishers. Her book was bought (and published in 1991) and—as I predicted—she had no trouble getting an agent.

Don't worry about an agent until you have a contract. *You* can do a far better job of pushing your first novel than any agent who's likely to be interested in you. But *do* get one before you sign on the dotted line. That's the point at which you'll get a decent agent. And they are worth their 10% (some, now, at 15%) to protect you from some nasty clauses.

• *Being Your Own Agent*

You won't need an agent for short story sales. Just make sure that you sell only one-time rights to a publication to use a story. Someday, you may want to resell that story. Payment, depending on what level you are at in your career, can range from a few copies of the magazine to 15 cents a word, and up. The SF magazines that publish the most SF generally pay between 6–8 cents a word.

If you get a publisher interested in your book, that is the time to call a few agents—listed in *Writer's Digest*—and see if one would be interested in handling the contract.

If you do go it alone, check out Richard Curtis's book on *How To Be Your Own Agent* or the *Science Fiction Writers Association Guide*. A first novel can bring the princely advance of $3000 with—on the average—a 6% royalty.

Make sure that the publisher only has an option— the right to make an offer—on your next *proposal*, not the completed book.

• Study the Field

And this doesn't just mean books in your area of interest, though that's important. It will be hard for you to craft an original story or novel without knowing what has come before. In the appendix, I list some recommended titles and authors, but these only scratch the surface. You need to haunt libraries and book stores, and study what's been done and what's being published.

If you try to absorb as much as you can, it will make your vision of your own work that much clearer.

Study the business end. Subscribe to *Locus* (34 Ridgewood Lane, Oakland, CA 94611) and *Science Fiction Chronicle* (P.O. Box 2730, Brooklyn, NY

11202–0056). These are magazines read by all the pros in the field.

Locus features a column by Richard Curtis, the agent of the Science Fiction Writers Association, and book reviews that will keep you on top of the field.

New releases are previewed, and conventions are listed for the coming year, complete with names of guests of honor, registration fees, and hotel information. There's also a section on which authors sold books recently, and to what publishing house. This can be vital information, alerting you to trends in the field, new editors, and new imprints.

Mystery Scene (3840 Clark Rd. S.E., Cedar Rapids, IA 52403) covers the related field of horror and dark fantasy, and is well worth picking up. Especially to read about authors commenting on their own adventures in publishing.

The Science Fiction Writers Association publishes *The Bulletin*, with market reports which you can get even if you're not a member. Valuable market information can also be found in the *Writer's Market*, an annual book, and *Writer's Digest* magazine.

Kathryn Ptacek publishes the *Gila Queen's Market Report*, perhaps the most valuable survey of who's buying what, from small press anthologies and magazines to the big publishing houses. The monthly list is available by subscription for $20 from Ptacek at: 28 Linwood Ave., Newton, NY 07860.

• *Learn the Business End*

Many authors I speak to complain about their lack of knowledge when they started, and how they took the first, and often worst, deal offered. Some had no idea how much their work was worth, or what contract clauses to watch out for.

There are some good books that will give you a thorough education in such business matters as how to avoid the deadly option clause and what a first novel is really worth. Stephen Goldin and Kathleen Skye's *The Business of Being a Writer* (Carroll & Graf) or Richard Curtis's *How to Be Your Own Agent* (Houghton-Mifflin) cover all the important topics.

The Science Fiction Writer's Association recently published the *Science Fiction Writers of America Handbook* (available from Writer's Notebook Press, Pulphouse Publishing, Box 1227, Eugene, OR 97440, for $10.00). Subtitled *The Professional Writer's Guide to Writing Professionally*, this is perhaps the most valuable book in the field, with chapters written by professional writers covering topics ranging from copyright law and negotiating to royalty statements and promotion.

It's an invaluable work and a must-have for your professional library.

• *Join Writers' Groups*

Investigate writers' groups in your area. Often, fiction groups will meet in a town's library. *Writer's Digest* magazine also lists, in an annual issue, writers' conferences, many devoted exclusively to science fiction and fantasy.

At such conferences, you can have your work critiqued and meet writers, editors, and agents. Sometimes, you can meet people with whom you can form a writers' group to meet informally when back home. This can be invaluable for supporting each other's work.

Professional groups can also be vital to helping you sell your work. The Science Fiction Writers of America (Executive Secretary, Peter D. Pautz, P.O. Box 4335, Spartanburg, SC 29305–4335) offer associate memberships which will bring you news of members and a magazine, *The Bulletin*, with market updates.

The Horror Writers of America (c/o Executive Secretary Leanne Johnson, P.O. Box 10901, Greensboro, NC 27404–0901) is a professional organization of horror and dark fantasy writers concerned with contracts, markets, and other professional matters. HWA also warns prospective authors away from less than scrupulous publishers. Current information about such companies can be found in the HWA newsletter.

• *Keep Writing*

While your chapters and outline are out in the marketplace, plan another novel, and go ahead and write that novel. When one story is making the rounds, keep track of it, but start *another*, perhaps targeted to different SF markets.

Keep working at the dozens of things talked about in these pages.

Until the moment comes when the world that you've made from scratch, the characters whose biographies you've invented, the multi-layered story you've planned, touches someone else's imagination, starting with an editor and, with a bit of magic and luck, thousands of readers . . .

Afterword

T HE future is nearly here. And here are two cases in point.

Recently, I finished a project for a division of Virgin Mastertronic, the computer game wing of the company that runs Virgin Airways, Virgin Pictures, and a host of other enterprises.

I wrote a 90-page script for a CD-ROM game, *Guest*, an exploration of a house besieged by forces from another galaxy. The producers aren't calling this a game. It's been dubbed a "Hypermovie." *Guest* will feature a cast of twelve actors, full motion video, stereophonic music and sound effects, and spoken dialogue and, believe me, you've never seen anything like it.

One major publisher has added a non-negotiable clause to the contracts that gives them control of what are called "electronic display rights." It appears that, in Japan, there is a small hand-held device that can display book text. It can search out chapters, charts, information. It holds your place so you can start from exactly where you left off.

And recently, *The New York Times* reported on Sony's plans to introduce the hand-held DataMan—a hand-held machine to display text from encyclopedias and other reference books. Eventually, such a device will have multimedia possibilities. Can books with sound effects and music, on a tiny disk, be far behind?

We want to be storytellers.

But just *how* we tell those stories may be changing in the decades to come.

And who better than SF writers to be in the forefront of the new technologies, finding new ways to tell tales?

Telling tales . . . speculative stories . . .

An activity that surely goes back to cold nights during the Ice Age, when people huddled near a fire and wondered about what was out there in the dark, or up there in the sky . . .

Appendix

A Recommended Reading List

The Foundation Trilogy—Isaac Asimov

Stranger in a Strange Land—Robert Heinlein

Childhood's End—Arthur C. Clarke

Lord Valentine's Castle—Robert Silverberg

The Lord of the Rings—J.R.R. Tolkien

Dandelion Wine—Ray Bradbury

The Stand—Stephen King

Dune—Frank Herbert

Eon—Greg Bear

The Shrinking Man—Richard Matheson

Make Room, Make Room!—Harry Harrison

When Gravity Fails—George Alec Effinger

Ender's Game—Orson Scott Card

Midnight—Dean R. Koontz

The Midwich Cuckoos—John Wyndham

Space Vampires—Colin Wilson

No Blade of Grass—John Christopher

For Your Professional Shelf

The Business of Being a Writer—Stephen Goldin and Kathleen Skye—Carroll & Graf

How to Be Your Own Agent—Richard Curtis—Houghton-Mifflin

How to Write Tales of Horror, Fantasy and Science Fiction—J. N. Williamson—Writer's Digest Books

Science Fiction Writers of America Handbook (available from Writer's Notebook Press, Pulphouse Publishing, Box 1227, Eugene, OR 97440 for $10.00)

Writer's Market 1992—Writer's Digest Press

A Selection of Magazines That Publish SF

Always read the magazine before attempting to submit a story. And always include a SASE for the return of your story.

Aboriginal Science Fiction—Charles C. Ryan, editor. 100 Tower Office Park, Suite K, Woburn, MA 01801.

Analog—Stanley Schmidt, editor. 380 Lexington Ave., New York, NY 10017.

Fear—John Gilbert, editor. Newsfield, Ludlow, Shropshire SY8 IJW, United Kingdom.

Interzone—David Pringle, editor. 124 Osborne Rd., Brighton BN1 6LU, United Kingdom.

Isaac Asimov's SF Magazine—Gardner Dozois, editor. 380 Lexington Ave., New York, NY 10017.

Fantasy & Science Fiction—Kristine Kathryn Rusch, editor. P.O. Box 11526, Eugene, OR 97440.

Marion Zimmer Bradley's Fantasy Magazine—Marion Zimmer Bradley, editor. P.O. Box 245–A, Berkeley, CA 94701.

Omni—Ellen Datlow, fiction editor. 1965 Broadway, New York, NY 10023–5965.

Weird Tales—George Scithers, editor. P.O. Box 13418, Philadelphia, PA 19101–3418.

A Selection of SF Novel Publishers

Avon Books—Editors: John Douglas, Marjorie Braman. The Hearst Book Group, 1350 Avenue of the Americas, New York, NY 10019.

Baen Books—Editor-in-Chief, Jim Baen. Distributed by Simon & Schuster, 260 Fifth Avenue, New York, NY 10001.

Bantam/Spectra—Editors, Amy Stout, Janna Silberstein. 666 Fifth Avenue, New York, NY 10103.

The Berkley Publishing Group—Editors, Peter Heck, Ginjer Buchanan. 200 Madison Avenue, New York, NY 10016.

Daw Books Inc.—Submissions Editor, Peter Stampfel, 1633 Broadway, New York, NY 10019.

Del Rey Books—Editor-in-Chief, Owen Lock, 201 E. 50th St., New York, NY 10022.

Harper Paperbacks—Editor, Carolyn Marino. 10 E. 53rd St., New York, NY 10022.

Pocket Books—Editors, John Scognamiglio, Sally Peters.

Simon & Schuster, 1230 Avenue of the Americas, New York, NY 10020.

ROC—New American Library—Editors, John Silbersack, Chris Schelling. 375 Hudson St., New York, NY 10014–3657.

Tor Books—Editor-in-Chief, Robert J. Gleason. 49 W. 24th St., New York, NY 10010.

Important SF Conventions in 1992

Boskone 29—February 14–16, Sheraton & Marriott, Springfield, MA. Guest of Honor, Jane Yolen. Write c/o NESFA, Box G, MIT, Br. PO, Cambridge, MA 02139–0910.

Lunacon '92—March 20–22. Guest of Honor, Samuel R. Delany. Rye Town Hilton, Rye Brook, NY. Write Box 338, New York, NY 10150–0338.

Magicon, 50th World SF Convention—September 3–7. Guest of Honor, Jack Vance. Orange County Civic & Convention Center, Orlando, FL. Write MagiCon, Box 621992, Orlando, FL 32862–1992.

World Fantasy Con—October 29–Nov. 1—Pine Mountain, GA. Box 148, Clarkston, GA 30021.

About the Author

MATTHEW J. COSTELLO is a Contributing Editor at *GAMES* magazine and a columnist for *Mystery Scene*. He has written for *Sports Illustrated, Writer's Digest*, and *Tower Video*. His interviews with Joan Rivers, Larry Hagman, Joel Silver, and others have appeared in *The Los Angeles Times* and *Amazing Stories* magazine.

His 1990 novel, *Midsummer*, was named one of the "Best Novels of 1990" by the Science Fiction Chronicle, as was *Beneath Still Waters* for the year 1989. LOCUS called Costello's latest horror novel, *WURM*, "A great book!" *WURM* was also a best-seller on the *Mystery Scene* list. His fantasy novel, *The Wizard of Tizare* (1990) was also a B. Dalton best-seller. His SF novel, *Time of the Fox*, launched his new time travel series for Penguin/ROC. Costello's mainstream thriller, *HOME*, will be a Berkley lead title for 1992.

In September of 1991, John Wiley & Sons published Matt Costello's new non-fiction book, *The Greatest Games of All Time*. His script for *GUEST*, a Virgin Software CD-ROM "Interactive Movie," will be filmed this fall with Vincent Price and a cast of twelve actors.

Costello lives in Ossining, New York, with his wife and three children.